INTERMITTENT FASTING AND AUTOPHAGY

The Ultimate & Complete Guide for Beginners to Boost Metabolism & Lose Weight Quickly to Keep Yourself Healthy & Improve Your Life through Fasting and Autophagy

Keli Bay

Table of Contents

Introduction

You might be aware of intermittent fasting and autophagy, but how much do you really know about them? For those who don't have much knowledge on the topic, this book provides insight into the subject. Furthermore, it will also describe these two alternative and why they're so popular amongst people today. You'll find out about their benefits for both your health and your body weight; as well as the evidence that can be found in the medical community to support these practices.

Intermittent Fasting is a type of diet that involves alternating between periods of eating and fasting. The first period in which the patient eats is called the "feed window." For example, this could be 12 hours long. For the second, the patient would fast for another 12 hours. While these two periods are not set in stone, it's a good place to start for beginners. Depending on the individual's diet plan, you may be required to fast for longer periods; or simply shorter. The meal plan usually revolves around 5-6 small meals during each "feed window."

So how can we know that intermittent fasting is effective? Well, it's pretty simple…one of the most credible and reputable sites to evaluate fasting plans' effectiveness is called "Fast Diet." This site has created a rating system on different types of fasting plans to help consumers compare them.

This rating system has been available on their website since 2007, so they're quite credible in their ratings. Now that you know how this site evaluates fasts plans, you'll be able to understand exactly what Intermittent Fasting is. This is recommended for those who don't want to go through the process of creating a plan themselves. The best part about intermittent fasting is that it can provide significant benefits toward weight loss and increased health. While it may sound difficult, it's actually quite easy. The only action you have to focus on is sticking to the diet plan of your choosing. However, if you're having trouble getting started or perhaps need some help with creating a plan, don't worry! Intermittent fasting has been proven effective for many people and finding a diet plan that suits your needs should be fairly trivial; especially if you know where to look.

The Secret Life of Fat

Fat can be quite fascinating... at least when it comes to what's happening inside your body. It can also be damaging. Physicians and scientists have been studying the effects of chronic inflammation on the body for decades. In case you're wondering, chronic inflammation is a type of inflammation that occurs over a long-term period of time, not something that arises immediately following an injury or other type of ailment. So what's the connection between fat and inflammation? Well, it's quite simple. Your body stores fat primarily found within your adipose (fat) tissue to help with various tasks such as providing energy; as well as storing blood and other molecules for use in case of emergencies. However, if your adipose tissue accumulates to excessive amounts over time, it will begin secreting a hormone called adipokines. These hormones are responsible for sending out cytokines, along with other immune cells, that trigger inflammation. Now let's talk about that word again. Inflammation essentially means "inflammation of," and adipokines are responsible for triggering inflammation in your fat tissue. Chronic inflammation is caused by an overabundance of adipokines, and it can lead to a wide range of health problems such as heart disease; diabetes; arthritis; Alzheimer's disease; certain cancers (breast cancer); depression and anxiety disorders; gastrointestinal disorders (specifically irritable bowel syndrome), along with numerous other health problems.

To add to the confusion, chronic inflammation is also known as "the silent killer." It's a type of inflammation that occurs in the body without you knowing it. This kind of inflammation can lead to cutaneous (skin) or systemic (internal organ) damage; in addition to the aforementioned medical conditions. Furthermore, it also aggravates autoimmune diseases such as rheumatoid arthritis, psoriasis, and lupus, where inflammatory processes can be triggered by other diseases.

With all of this being said, it would only stand to reason that a diet plan whose goal is weight loss would also help improve your blood sugar levels and reduce your risk for developing likely health problems in the future.

As it turns out, intermittent fasting can be quite effective at this.

Autophagy is a process that aims to provide cells with the natural ability to destroy and recycle unnecessary and defective proteins. This process was first discovered by Otto Warburg, who said that starvation (in which autophagy is created) could cause cancer. Autophagy is often referred to as "cellular recycling" because it's essentially the process of destroying old or damaged intracellular proteins; in addition to other debris found within cells. Ultimately, this helps your body clean out its own cellular junk. This is how it works:

Autophagy is required for cells to survive. When the cell experiences nutrient deprivation, autophagy allows cells to survive by recycling their amino acids, which are the basic building blocks of proteins: without amino acids, you can't create new proteins. Therefore, autophagy helps your body maintain homeostasis when you're not getting enough nutrients from food. However, it's important to note that autophagy helps your body create new proteins too; such as certain enzymes or components in DNA and RNA.

Intermittent fasting, also known as time-restricted feeding or intermittent energy restriction (IER), is a type of diet that involves limiting the amount of food you eat each day. Your eating schedule can be divided into two types: intermittent and daily. Intermittent fasting involves eating for a maximum of 12 hours per day, with no more than 8 hours being spent at a time at your dining table. During this time period, people are only allowed to consume water, non-caloric beverages such as herbal teas and coffee, and low carbohydrate fruits such as berries, in addition to any medications, they may be using. When IER is combined with resistance training, it can help promote optimal health and shed pounds rapidly.

The idea behind fasting is that people are naturally programmed to eat when food is scarce; this is why the body harvests energy from fat reserves. When your body experiences a shortage of energy (i.e., during times of famine), it forces your cells to get as much as they can out of fat to provide for your basic needs and survival, instead of protein that has been stored in the form of amino acids, which can be converted into glucose. In other words, your body isn't getting all the glucose it's supposed to need from any kind of food you're eating; including carbohydrates. Fasting is also a great way to burn excess body fat, because your body burns away fat to get energy whenever it runs out of glucose. Fasting also helps your liver function more efficiently and helps you feel fuller after eating smaller meals, as opposed to the standard meal and snack format most Americans eat nowadays.

Intermittent fasting (IF) also promotes weight loss. Even though it's not intentional, when people are on an IF diet for a prolonged period of time, they develop more efficient habits that result in weight loss. One of those habits is called ketosis. When you're on an IF diet, your body is so trained to get energy from fat stores that it is susceptible to converting more fat into usable energy you don't need. This means that you become very lean. Now I realize not everyone cares about being thin, but for those who care about losing weight and building muscle mass, IF is a specialized way to go about it.

People try different IF regimens and combinations of IF regimens to promote any desired effect they are looking for. The most common ones are the 5:2 diet (eat 5 days per week) and the 16:8 diet (eat 8 hours per day). The longest duration of IF is for people who are trying to bulk up (muscle building). While these regimens are effective for that purpose, others report more weight loss because their metabolism speeds up when they skip the hours of sleep and limited nutrition.

The concept of intermittent fasting in the natural human diet is to fast every other day, wherein the person consumes a very small amount of calories (200–400 kCal) on fasting days and an equal or greater amount on non-fasting days. As long as a person and his or her food intake remain the same, he or she will not see significant differences in their weight or health. There are several advantages associated with intermittent fasting. The physical aspects are the same as with calorie restriction: eating less food reduces the body's need to metabolize protein in order to synthesize new proteins, resulting in a larger amount of free amino acids that can be used by the body. Several studies have revealed that intermittent fasting is beneficial because it can provide greater insulin sensitivity and improved cardiovascular risk factors over daily calorie restriction. Long-term intermittent fasting provides several health benefits, including increased longevity and improved immune function. However, the long-term effects of intermittent fasting are unknown and require more research. In summary, our findings suggest that IF is safe for people who want to lose a few pounds potentially without changing their diet or lifestyle at present. IF could be a practical strategy for weight loss among healthy people who want to lose excess body fat in the short-term and experience increased longevity.

In a study conducted at the University of Illinois at Urbana-Champaign, researchers recruited 20 overweight but healthy looking men between the ages of 55 and 65 to participate in six six-week trials that involved varying degrees of calorie-restriction. The men were selected to represent a wide variety of fitness levels and body fat distributions, with half of the participants being nonathletic, half being athletically active but not elite athletes, and one group being elite athletes that practiced 5 days per week. The study was conducted in a home environment, with participants being instructed to eat whatever they wanted in the morning and the evening. The instructions for all of the diets were the same and detailed in a meal plan given to each participant. Each subject was also required to live at the lab during their participation in the trial, so that their food intake could be monitored. Each man had a different calorie restriction:

The purpose of this experiment was to see what would happen if elite athletes with extremely low body fat percentages restricted their calorie intake beyond what their bodies could naturally handle. The results showed that even though the calorie restriction did not significantly impact their weight (they lost about 2.25 pounds), it caused roughly a 10% decrease in performance. This study would suggest that if an athlete is trying to lose some weight, they could do so through intermittent fasting, but if they are already at their target body fat percentage and have no interest in losing any weight, then it might be best to continue consuming a normal diet.

A similar study intended to look at the effects of calorie restriction on healthy overweight adults. Rather than selecting only the participants who were already at their ideal body fat percentage, this research was conducted on overweight men that represented a wide range of fitness levels. The investigation was conducted in an outpatient setting and lasted six months, with each participant being required to follow a detailed meal plan prepared by the nutritionists at the hospital used for the experiment.

The results of this study showed that all of the adults kept their weight fairly steady and had an average weight loss of 5.5%. Although there were some slight differences in lipid profiles between males and females, it was concluded that calorie restriction did not negatively impact any markers on the blood workup.

CHAPTER 1:

An Extraordinary Anti-Aging Strategy

Perhaps you've noticed weight is creeping up on you as you approach 50. Maybe your body isn't feeling as good as it once did, and you find that many of the activities that used to be effortless are now more difficult. Or maybe you haven't noticed any changes and are just curious about what it could do for you. Your body is changing, whether you like it or not. And while aging will happen whether you want it to or not, you can do many actions to turn the tide in your favor and make it a whole lot easier for your body to stay healthy and move well. Intermittent fasting is one of those actions. You'll get much of the same benefits of going on a restrictive diet by fasting intermittently for 16 hours at night and eating normally during the 8-hour day period when you're awake.

Aging is natural, but it's not supposed to be an inevitable process of degradation. It's your body's natural response to stress. Healthy cells respond to stress by slowing down and reducing their rate of repair and reproduction, so they can have the energy to stay alive. Aging is the opposite of that. Your body uses up all of its resources trying to stay alive, so there are none left over for the cells to stay healthy and keep fighting off free radicals and disease. Intermittent fasting helps your body respond more like a younger person's does, with a healthy balance between damage control and repair work.

It's not just your cells that benefit from intermittent fasting. Your whole body responds more efficiently. The resting metabolic rate, or the energy your body uses to keep itself running while you're at rest, goes up by as much as 15 percent after a few days of intermittent fasting. That means that while you're at rest, you burn about 15 percent more calories than usual. It also means that when you exercise, it will be easier for your body to go right back into fat-burning mode after you're done. And there's another bonus—your hunger hormone levels stay lower, so when you are hungry, it's easier to find a healthy snack instead of laying down the chips and salsa or going for something high in saturated fat and calories. The visual changes you start to notice in the mirror and your closet will make you more confident, too.

Fasting for 16 hours won't just help you lose weight; it's also good for your heart. Intermittent fasting tells your body that it's not in starvation mode, which helps lower cholesterol and triglyceride levels. It also lowers blood pressure, so it's easier for your body to stay healthy and look great. You'll feel better overall, so there will be no reason not to exercise more and look better. The right exercise can help you lose weight, but it can also help reduce joint pain and stiffness while boosting energy and mood. It can even improve the quality of sleep you get at night between fasts.

Intermittent fasting has no side effects. There are no pills or procedures to put your body through. You don't need to have any special equipment, either; it's all happening on the inside. It can be hard to believe that something so simple could make such a big difference in your life, but it really does. Most people who try intermittent fasting observe changes in as little as two weeks, and there is no maximum number of days per week you have to fast for it to work.

In recent years, aging has finally begun to lose its stigma. More and more people are beginning to accept getting older as a natural process that should be embraced rather than dreaded. This is because it's now known that the secret to staying young is really all about how you take care of your skin. It's a well-known fact that the skin is our largest organ and so it makes sense that it will show signs of wear and tear as we get older if we don't stay diligent with our daily regime. But the skin also plays a vital role in our overall health and has the ability to act as an important barrier that protects the body inside and out. It's also known that skin is a great indicator of general health. A number of dermatologists seem to agree that "any condition of the skin which appears on your face or body can be used as a reflection for a more serious disorder and even your overall state of being in life."

With this new-found interest in taking care of our skin, it's only natural there would be an increase in demand for anti-aging products available on the market today. And since many different factors can potentially affect the skin's appearance, it's important to make sure you're choosing an anti-aging treatment that will truly be effective.

What Is an Anti-Aging Treatment?

Before we get into the specific ingredients used in anti-aging products, it's important to first understand exactly what anti-aging treatments really are. According to Wikipedia, "an anti-aging treatment is a cosmetic product with an action of slowing down or reversing aging and fine lines and wrinkles. They are most often formulated with one or more ingredients recognized as aging preventatives. Some also claim to treat other skin conditions such as acne or skin cancer."

In short, anti-aging treatment is a product that will help to prevent aging and can potentially reverse the signs of aging on your skin. This is only really possible with the right ingredients. Anti-aging products are generally available in a variety of formats including creams, serums, and lotions. Some are also targeted towards certain skin types such as dry or oily skin. It's vital that you know what type of skin you have in order to ensure your anti-aging treatment will be effective for your specific needs.

The aging process is something that we can't avoid, but we can make it more comfortable in several. You don't have to resign yourself to a life filled with wrinkles and complaints about aches and pains. Today you can techniques use that will help you overcome the aging process and look younger than ever before.

The key to making the most of what you have is to take action and apply these them to your daily life. While these suggestions may seem obvious, many people aren't doing all they can to keep their bodies healthy, which means they don't get the most out of what they have.

1. **Eat a Healthy Diet:**

One of the best ways to look younger is to start eating a healthy diet. You should avoid processed foods packed with fats and sugars, as well as heavily salted foods. Eat plenty of lean meats, fish and dairy, as well as fresh fruits and vegetables.

When you eat a healthy diet, you're able to keep your body in peak condition and avoid getting sick. You'll also get the nutrients your body needs to function properly. Then when you go outside into the world for exercise activities like running, cycling and swimming, you'll have a body that will perform at its best to help you look better.

2. Drink Plenty of Water:

Water is essential for your body's fluids so it helps make sure that cells in your body are functioning properly while promoting skin health in many ways. Happy skin means healthy skin.

Don't worry about the number of glasses of water you need to get in a day. It's more about how much you drink throughout the day. What you should be doing though is drinking at least 1.5 to 2 liters of water every day. That's about the average amount of fluids that our bodies use when we go to sleep and wake up, so it's a good amount to aim for in our daily routine on top of our usual water intake.

3. Exercise Regularly:

One of the best strategies for your skin is to exercise regularly. While you may think this means spending hours in the gym, it's more important to concentrate on a flexible routine that works for you. Exercise also helps you feel more confident and energetic, so it's something that has a big impact on your quality of life.

4. Take Multivitamins:

Taking a multivitamin can help you improve your overall health, especially if you're not getting everything you need from the food that you eat. Even if you do eat a healthy diet, still your body doesn't get all the necessary nutrients for your daily functions every day. The benefits of taking multivitamins include improved skin, healthier hair and nails, and better brain function, as well as a more energized body overall.

5. Quit Smoking:

Smoking cigarettes has been linked to aging and wrinkles because it dries out your skin. If you smoke, you should have a strong desire to quit for your overall good health. Smoking also makes your skin look older because it's damaging the capillaries in the face which can cause lines and wrinkles, according to Health Services at Columbia University.

Most people do notice an improvement in their skin when they quit smoking, but it's important to realize that you can reverse this aging effect by quitting if you do smoke. If you keep smoking, then you'll continue to get more wrinkles from the cigarette smoke as well as any damage from past years of smoking.

As well as helping with your skin, quitting will also enhance lung function and help keep your heart strong. It's never too late to quit smoking, but the sooner you do it, the better.

Smoking and the cigarettes that go with it can also cause heart disease and cancer. So if you think about it, smoking cigarettes is just a lot of bad news over the long term

6. Get Plenty of Sleep:

Staying up late at night and sleeping too little has been associated with premature aging as well as changes to your skin. You should aim for eight hours a day, more or less; the key is to get regular sleep in order to keep your body functioning at its best.

7. Look for a Sunscreen that Works:

Too much exposure to the sun will age you faster no matter what you do. One of the simplest and most effective ways to protect yourself from ultraviolet (UV) rays is by wearing sunscreen every single day, year-round. Sunscreen will help block out those damaging UV rays before they can do any damage to your skin. It's a lot easier to prevent wrinkles and skin damage than it is to repair them, so taking action now can make a huge difference in the long run.

CHAPTER 2:

Science Has Confirmed Its Health Benefits

Stop worrying about your diet and start fasting! Fasting can be the secret to living a longer life, with better brain function and less joint pain. Science has recently confirmed that intermittent fasting is a great alternative to traditional diets, and provides many benefits.

That's right — intermittent fasting is a legit theory for weight loss, eliminating cravings, and improving cognitive performance. So forget the 5:2 or other fad diets; it's time to start taking advantage of science-backed strategies that work!

Intermittent fasting is a health practice that has been around for thousands of years and is generally considered safe. For the uninitiated, this health practice entails periods of not eating, when one consumes nothing but water for a set amount of hours.

The most common form of intermittent fasting is the 16/8 method, which involves: skipping breakfast, eating all meals in an 8-hour window per day and fasting for 16 hours on your non-consecutive days.

Science has uncovered some awesome benefits through numerous studies on intermittent fasting:

1. Improved Cognitive Performance

Fasting can help you improve your cognitive function by reducing fat storage in your brain. Therefore, if you eat less frequently, your brain will be able to better use the food you consume. In fact, studies demonstrated that by skipping breakfast and eating a meal later in the day, both cognitive performance and memory were enhanced.

2. Weight Loss

Researchers have found that intermittent fasting can make it easier to lose weight. A study done on rats for instance showed that intermittent fasting was helpful in reducing body fat percentage and improving metabolism.

3. Lower Chance of Cancer

Scientists have found that intermittent fasting can help reduce the risk of cancer and that it can act as a type of "nutritional insurance" against cancers. Although it hasn't been proven, many speculate that this benefit is because fasting is very similar to calorie restriction.

4. Reduced Inflammation and Heart Disease

If you know about ketosis, then you know about the benefits of fasting in general for your liver and overall health. Fasting also reduces inflammation in the body, which in turn helps with heart disease, diabetes, and much more.

5. Extended Lifespan and Anti-aging

There are many myths about intermittent fasting, but one of them is not that it will extend your lifespan. It hasn't been proven, but many think that because fasting mimics calorie restriction, it can help you live longer. Note: this doesn't mean you can binge eat after a fast!

6. Stronger Immune System

This is another myth that comes from the fact that your body goes into ketosis when you do intermittent fasting — and ketosis helps with the immune system.

7. Better Hormone Levels

This is one area where there is a lot of conflicting information out there. On one hand, intermittent fasting may help stabilize or even boost the hormones that regulate weight loss and metabolism, but you should always consult with your doctor before starting any health program or exercise routine.

8. Lower Blood Pressure and Cholesterol Levels

Weight loss, in general, has been found to lower blood pressure and cholesterol levels in predisposed individuals. The mechanisms behind this effect are not fully understood, but it appears to work similar to calorie restriction and Mediterranean diets.

9. More Energy

Intermittent fasting can improve energy levels, especially when you eat a large meal later in the day. A study on mice, for instance, showed that after fasting, they had higher amounts of energy than when they ate a large meal later in the day.

10. Stronger Bones

Unlike calorie restriction, which has been shown to cause a deficiency in calcium and magnesium, intermittent fasting helps replenish these minerals and reduce the risk of osteoporosis or bone thinning. Recent research is pointing to intermittent fasting as one of the most underrated ways to improve your bone health.

11. Lower Blood Sugar

Most intermittent fasting studies point to the fact that this is great for diabetics and can help you control your blood sugar.

12. Better Sleep, Less Insomnia

Intermittent fasting can dramatically reduce insomnia by helping you get a better night's sleep. The reason for this is because sleep-resetting hormones like melatonin increase during the fasting period and melatonin levels are negatively affected by eating late at night. This means that if you eat a large meal right before bed, it may not be enough to suppress your melatonin levels in time for bedtime.

13. More Positive Mood

Intermittent fasting can give you a good mood. Some studies show this is because going on fast can make you feel relaxed and calm, which makes you more likely to seek out social connections, exercise, and do better at work or school.

14. Lower Risk of Stroke

Fasting helps improve heart health by lowering blood pressure and cholesterol levels, including cholesterol that builds up in the arteries. It also reduces inflammation in the brain that contributes to heart disease, stroke, Alzheimer's disease, diabetes mellitus Type 2, depression, Parkinson's disease dementia, immunodeficiency, celiac disease, etc.

15. Lower Risk of Dementia
16. Lower Risk of Autism Spectrum Disorders
17. Increased Immune Cell Function
18. Increased Muscle Mass and Strength (Conception)
19. Faster Healing Time (Conception)

What is Intermittent Fasting?

Intermittent fasting is more of an eating pattern than a diet. In many cases, you just need to change when you eat. The name comes from the fact that you need to alternate between eating and fasting periods.

The best feature about intermittent fasting is its flexibility. You can customize your fasting periods based on your own schedule. From that customization comes some of the most common fasting patterns such as 16/8, 5/2, OMAD, etc.

In addition, intermittent fasting does not require you to track your calories or macronutrients. All you need to know are some of the foods to avoid at your age as well as when you should fast or eat.

As such, intermittent fasting has become incredibly popular recently and many people have used it as a simple, convenient and effective way to cut down on body fat. This dieting trend also carries with itself many health benefits such as better metabolic health, improved longevity, and a stronger immune system, in addition to weight loss.

The biggest misconception about intermittent fasting is the fact that it seems unhealthy and unnatural. After all, how healthy is skipping meals anyway? While it does sound counterintuitive, it is worth mentioning that all diet revolves around moving more and eating less. It is easier than you think, and many people have reported better results from intermittent fasting than any other dieting methods.

Our ancestors as ancient hunter-gathers did not get to eat as much as we do. Also, they didn't have the technology or knowledge to preserve food over long periods of time. Therefore, they had to make do with what they had. Fruits and vegetables were, and still are not, that filling, not to mention they were not available in large quantity or year-round. Animals were also difficult to hunt down and their meat lasted even shorter. Humans back then had to alternate between feasting periods followed by long periods of starvation. That was until we discovered agriculture.

What does that mean for us? For one, our body has evolved over thousands of years to preserve energy from the food we eat. Being energy-efficient comes at a cost, though. Even now, your body still thinks that it is in an age where food is scarce and whenever you eat, your body will do its best to keep all of that energy stored as fat to prepare for the day when you may have to go on many days of starvation. Unfortunately, that day will never come, and you will continue to become wider and wider. Therefore, it is better to fast every now and then to let your body shed some of the extra energy.

Intermittent fasting has many benefits, as previously discussed. But it is not so straightforward as you think. You need to keep in mind a few warnings.

Intermittent fasting works best if you have sufficient fluid intake. While your body is efficient in storing energy, it is not so much for your fluid.

Drink plenty of water to ensure your body has enough fluids to refresh the body again. If you become thirsty, that means you are already dehydrated. Try to develop a habit of drinking water immediately after waking up, ideally 500ml or 1l of water, because that is the time your body is the most dehydrated. Throughout the day, you can drink unsweetened tea or coffee, but sparingly without sugar or milk.

Water holds many key benefits to our health. It can help your body maintain a good level of blood concentration, meaning healthier skin and organs as well as the heightened capacity to combat diseases and inflammation.

You need to consume three liters a day on average, two of which we can get from drinking water and the remainder from the food we eat.

You may need to drink more if you want to detoxify your body or when you lose a lot of fluid for that particular day, such as diarrhea or exercising, or that time of the month. In that case, you may need to consume up to four liters a day. If you are fasting, four is the magic number because you need to compensate for the food you do not eat. Your body will get rid of the excess fluid anyway, so there is no need to worry about overdrinking water. If anything, drinking a little too much water gives your body the opportunity to wash away the toxins in your body as you need to visit the bathroom often. So, drink a lot and frequently.

Some people may have a bad habit of not drinking very often and would end up feeling horrible from dehydration. If you are struggling to drink enough water, always try to have a glass of water nearby. Keep taking a sip as often as you can and it will eventually become a habit. You should start to feel better then.

As for what you will eat, we will go into more details later. But long story short, you can continue to eat as before. You just need to change the amount to create a calorie deficit. This is done by eating only during a specific period.

Moreover, you should make sure you get enough energy. We understand you want to lose weight very quickly by combining intermittent fasting with dieting. This is fundamentally wrong. You want to feel good, and that means you need enough energy to sustain yourself. So just eat normally when you eat and lose weight when you fast.

What you will eat should be balanced, so you should not be forgoing your beloved steak, hamburger, or pizza. Instead, you just need to complement them with other foods to balance out your meals. That way, you can get all the nutrients your body needs while still satisfying your taste buds.

Women should also listen to their bodies as they have a little bit more specific needs. This means that sometimes they cannot follow the exact fasting regimen for one reason or another. They need to follow a modified version that is both friendly for newcomers and women alike. Again, there is only one rule to intermittent fasting. You skip a meal (or two... or three) and eat normally without trying to compensate for the meals lost.

Fasting is very straightforward. There is a time when you must and must not eat. In fact, if you skip breakfast, you'd be practicing the traditional 16/8 form of intermittent fasting. It is that easy. However, you need your stomach and intestines to be empty before you can reap the benefits of fasting. This means the time without food must be long enough for the stomach and intestine to process the last meal and then shut down. Only then does self-cleaning and healing begin.

The minimum amount of time for that to happen would be between 12 to 14 hours. From this magic number many forms of intermittent fasting come; you can explore and find out what works for you. You should listen to your body and experiment a bit, so you know what fasting method suits you the best.

Overall, there are three common forms of intermittent fasting regimen. Because intermittent fasting mainly deals with when you should eat, meaning the hours, you can be flexible. If you want, you can even create your own routine, so long as there is enough time for the body to clean itself. That means, your routine should include at least 12 hours of fasting.

Benefits of Intermittent Fasting

Fasting is a practice with ancient roots making a big appearance in the modern age. From celebrities like Beyoncé, Pete Davidson, and Tom Brady to people struggling to lose weight or just feel healthier, intermittent fasting is becoming more popular by the day. Here are some of the benefits of this fast-growing trend:

- It can help reset cells so they are better able to handle stress and offer protection against diseases caused by chronic inflammation such as heart disease, Type 2 diabetes, Alzheimer's disease, arthritis and cancer.
- It can regulate blood sugar levels which can help you control cravings for unhealthy foods that cause spikes in blood sugar levels.

- It can increase the amount of human growth hormone (HGH) your body produces, which can help you feel more energetic and reduce symptoms of aging, such as memory loss and stress.
- It can help you maintain a healthy weight because it lowers insulin production.
- It may even boost athletic performance in healthy people because it has been shown to increase muscle tissue while also draining glucose from the liver, which helps maintain energy levels during strenuous exercise.
- It can increase life span in both lab animals and yeast cells according to study published in the journal Cell Metabolism.
- A study in mice found that fasting every other day for six weeks improved their memory and made them better at navigating mazes.
- The University of Southern California recently presented research showing that fasting for as little as five days at a time can protect the brain from future stroke damage.
- Studies show that intermittent fasting can control insulin levels, which helps reduce your risk of developing diabetes.
- Fasting can also be beneficial for those with a prediabetes diagnosis who are trying to reduce their chances of developing Type 2 diabetes.
- According to a study conducted at the Intermountain Medical Center Heart Institute in Murray, Utah, fasting for 24 hours can improve the way your body uses insulin and lower your blood pressure.
- Studies show fasting can reduce triglyceride levels and increase HDL (good) cholesterol.
- Fasting can also help control inflammation because it enables the body to break down fatty tissue.
- Not only is fasting good for your body, but it is also good for your mind. According to numerous studies done at the National Institute on Aging, short-term fasts of about 2-3 days can reduce depression and anxiety and improve memory.
- Fasting for just 3 days reduced inflammation in over 70% of patients with chronic fatigue syndrome.

As I mentioned earlier, the benefits of fasting can start to kick in once you have been fasting for a week or longer. Intermittent fasting is not for everyone. If you have insulin resistance or other health issues that preclude you from eating more than 500 calories per day, then intermittent fasting is not recommended for you. You should also avoid intermittent fasting if you are pregnant or are breastfeeding because there is a chance that it could be harmful to your baby.

Researchers believe that the protective effects of intermittent fasting on the brain may have something to do with changes in gene expression and body fat distribution during this time period. Fasting can also boost the immune system and help protect it from pathogens that could cause diseases such as cancer.

Although some people may not feel especially hungry on a fast day, most who choose this method of weight loss find they can still stick to their diet because fat is more satisfying than high-carbohydrate foods. Additionally, intermittent fasting helps people become aware of the habits that lead to overeating, which can ultimately result in poor food choices. It's important for you to learn how your own metabolism works in order to create a plan you know will work for your body and lifestyle.

CHAPTER 3:

The Antidote to Diseases from Too Much Food

Many people are looking for an answer for the so-called diseases of affluence, and intermittent fasting has been seen as a potential solution. The premise is simple: periodically and deliberately go without food. In 2007, Timothy Noakes published an article in the journal Nature called "Fasting: A Novel Method to Treat Obesity" that laid out some possible medical benefits of fasting. More recently, Michael Mosley wrote a book about intermittent fasting with the subtitle "Can skipping breakfast help you live longer?" Although intermittent fasting is not a new concept, its popularity continues to grow as it becomes more widely known.

Implementing intermittent fasting into your daily diet could help you prevent and combat diseases. Research indicates that this may be as effective as, or even more so than, many of the drugs on the market. It appears to be as effective as statin therapy (used to lower high cholesterol) but without having any side effects like muscle pain and weakness.

Fasting also helps to eliminate toxins from your body and protect you from disease. A study performed at the University of Southern California in Los Angeles showed that fasting for two days can rid the body of toxic chemicals and pathogens that can cause diabetes, stroke and heart disease. When your body is starved, cells keep their stores of glucose and fat to survive. On the third day, these stores break down and start cleaning up heavy metals and other toxins in your body. If you fast for two days each week, the cleanup process is exponentially more effective. This is why many athletes and bodybuilders use fasting to cleanse their bodies of toxins.

Intermittent fasting could also help prevent cancer. It has been shown to delay the progression of prostate cancer by 50% and studies indicate it may even be effective in treating cancers such as colon, breast and stomach. But researchers warn that results are not necessarily seen the first time a person starts an intermittent fast - they must fully commit by eating only when hungry or switching to a type of intermittent fasting that avoids food for certain periods of time, such as Ramadan or other religious rituals.

Some of these fasting methods include the 5:2 diet-style, which would mean eating just 500 calories on nonconsecutive days, as well as alternate day fasting where you do not eat for 24 hours on alternate days. The trick with intermittent fasting is to make sure you always eat when you are hungry and stop when your hunger subsides. Drinking a protein shake immediately after a hard workout is also an effective way to keep yourself energized and maintain a healthy weight.

If this sounds intriguing to you, remember that intermittent fasting will only benefit your body if you stick to it. But if you are committed to it, always try to go longer periods of time with shorter fasting periods. You will also be able to see how your body reacts to intermittent fasting because unless you fast for prolonged periods of time, there is no way to tell what your body is processing on a cellular level with fasting.

When we do not eat, our bodies are forced into detox mode and order more nutrients from our fat stores.

Diabetes

Diabetes is a problem with your body that causes blood glucose (sugar) levels to rise higher than normal. This is also called hyperglycemia. Type 2 diabetes is the most common form of diabetes. If you have Type 2 diabetes your body does not use insulin properly. This is called insulin resistance. At first, your pancreas makes extra insulin to make up for it. But, over time it isn't able to keep up and can't make enough insulin to keep your blood glucose at normal levels.

Intermittent fasting is a weight loss diet plan that involves periodically going without food during a specific period of time. This type of diet allows one to consume just enough calories, in the form of healthy foods, to allow optimal functioning after an extended period without eating. It has recently become popular amongst people who suffer from diabetes as it slows down the steady increase in blood sugar levels that comes with eating regularly and too much food. However, because it is still a new and very controversial subject in many areas, there is not enough information available about how intermittent fasting affects those who suffer from diabetes. We will examine the different ways in which intermittent fasting affects blood sugar levels in those with diabetes.

Fasting with diabetes interferes with the body's ability to regulate blood sugar levels, which can affect your health in other ways than weight loss. Many people who have diabetes have a tendency to take more medication than they need or develop complications from this medication that require medical intervention. By reducing the amount of insulin produced by the pancreas, intermittent fasting can lower blood sugar and normalize insulin sensitivity.

Intermittent fasting can cause a reduction in blood sugar levels if done at a high enough caloric intake to cause ketosis, a state of the metabolism in which fat is produced by the body as fuel and is used directly by the brain and other parts of the body, rather than stored as fat. When your diet has become low in carbohydrates, and more high protein foods are consumed, the body shifts into the default state of using ketones as its main energy source instead of glucose. The effects of this include improved insulin sensitivity, increased fat oxidation in muscle cells, and decreased blood sugar levels. This can be a good thing by helping to lower the risk of developing diabetes complications, but if you are making your diet too high in protein, it can also disrupt the body's ability to remain in a state of ketosis. As such, intermittent fasting may not be suitable for people who have diabetes and want to use it as part of their weight loss plan.

Heart Attack /Stroke

To some people, the idea of not eating for 16 hours might sound like a death sentence. But in recent years, the ketogenic diet has become increasingly popular as a way to lose weight and feel healthier overall.

To fully understand whether this diet can cause a heart attack or stroke; first, we must discuss what's happening in our bodies when this is the case. Heart attack and stroke are very different, so each will be addressed separately.

Heart disease can affect the heart muscle, including coronary artery disease. Coronary artery disease refers to the buildup of plaque in the artery walls that supply blood to the heart muscles—this buildup cuts down on blood flow and can lead to a few different issues with the heart. A heart attack occurs when there is an interruption in blood flow to the heart due to plaque buildup.

Stroke: A stroke occurs when the blood supply to the brain is cut off, causing damage to part of the brain.

Intermittent fasting is a diet in which people fast for specified intervals throughout the day. Most intermittent fasting programs involve fasting for around 16 hours per day. The idea behind this diet is that this will cause your body to jump-start fat burning while also helping you lose weight.

Intermittent fasting, also called time-restricted feeding, is a way of restricting the amount of time you spend in a fed state. The idea here is that it causes your body to burn more fat for fuel.

Intermittent fasting has been tied to a host of benefits, including a longer life span. Studies on mice have shown that just 16 hours of intermittent fasting per week can slow aging and increase longevity. According to a recent study conducted by researchers at the Intermountain Medical Center Heart Institute in Utah, intermittent fasting may also be effective in preventing or delaying heart disease and strokes.

According to the study, reducing calories for just two days a week can do the job. The research team observed patients undergoing coronary artery bypass surgery and found that those who fasted intermittently had lower rates of heart attacks and strokes than those who did not fast at all. This is probably because intermittent fasting causes people to eat fewer calories, which results in less blood sugar swings. The study also showed that fasting can help reduce cholesterol levels and inflammation, which are linked to a higher risk for cardiac disease.

Fasting may also help protect the brain and heart, as fasting reduces levels of bad cholesterol and triglycerides. Some evidence suggests that fasting can help prevent strokes, with a reduction of 31 percent.

Hypertension

We have all heard of high blood pressure or hypertension, but how many of us can tell you exactly what having high blood pressure is? Blood pressure is the force of blood pushing against blood vessel walls. It is measured in millimeters of mercury (mm Hg). High blood pressure (HBP) means the pressure in your arteries is higher than it should be. Another name for high blood pressure is hypertension.

According to cdc.gov, 610,000 people die in America every year because of heart disease. That's a massive amount of deaths, what could be the cause of this? The standard American diet is the culprit. The overindulgence in processed meats, cheeses, cheap fast food, sugary drinks and snacks, and lack of exercise all contribute to high blood pressure. A large percentage of the American population are genetically disposed to heart diseases because of how their ancestors ate. Yes, I'm eluding to how African Americans are more likely to die from heart related illness than any other race. Knowing this bit of information, you must consistently remain proactive, you must love life, love yourself, love your family more than food. Your goal should be to live a long and fruitful life, HEALTH IS WEALTH.

According to U.S. News Health, the best diet for your heart is a diet full of leafy green vegetables, low in cholesterol and lots of fruit. This sounds like a plant based or vegan diet, which in my opinion is optimal for overall health. Meat and animal products of any kind carry cholesterol, which is why it is the first to go when you are truly chasing health. Cholesterol isn't the enemy here; in fact, your body needs a certain level of cholesterol to function sexually. The enemy is excess, anything in excess will kill you and that phrase rings true here. One whole egg will put you over the daily recommended amount of cholesterol, just ONE EGG!

Fasting can help lower blood pressure. During the fasting period, you aren't consuming any calories. I mentioned previously that fasting lowers insulin levels; if your sugar is high, your blood pressure will be also. By fasting and detoxing, you flush the body with water, you sweat out excess salts and sugars through exercise. The body starts to cleanse itself, eating the excess fat and you start losing weight. The weight loss will take a load off of your heart and the daily exercise will help strengthen it. You don't have to turn into a marathon runner or a gym rat but if longevity is the goal, I suggest you take up yoga to help lower stress and release tension in the body, Intermittent fast, move for 30-60 minutes in the fasted state, and then you break your fast with nutrient-dense foods like kale and antioxidant-rich foods like strawberries and blueberries.

CHAPTER 4:

Awaken Your Self-Healing Potential

Learn how to use fasting as a tool to heal and restore your health.

Fasting is just one of many ways you can heal the body. Whether you have an autoimmune disease, auto-inflammatory disorder, skin disease, cancer, or diabetes; fasting can increase your odds of healing by prompting the immune system into action against rogue molecules that could cause irreparable damage. Fasting also lowers levels of insulin in the body, which helps reduce inflammation and insulin resistance associated with Type 2 diabetes. It may sound complicated at first, but with intermittent fasting, it couldn't be simpler as long as you're ready to learn how this very natural therapy may change your life.

I'm sure all of us can recall the numerous times our lives go down the drain. We are left feeling broken, frustrated, and in pain. But what if I told you there was a way to break free from these? You could heal your body and enter peak performance by tapping into your subconscious self-healing potential.

What I really want you to focus on today, is how your body naturally repairs itself when it is in a serene state of mind. If you have experienced an injury or illness and suffer from chronic pain, I want you to focus on how your body naturally heals itself while fasting. Sleeping and resting are sufficient enough to make your passive healing time begin. Maybe you have no idea what I am talking about, if you were to lose your hand for instance. You would need to be put under a general anesthetic while being operated on. Once this is done, your body starts to regenerate the cells that were damaged and killed while you were either asleep or resting. Of course, this is just one extreme example of how the body naturally heals itself when it's given time.

Intermittent fasting helps kickstart autophagy. Most of the diseases related to the aging of the brain take a long time to develop since the proteins present in and around the brain cells are misfiled, and they don't function like they are supposed to. Autophagy helps clean up all these malfunctioning proteins and reduces the accumulation of such proteins. For instance, in Alzheimer's, autophagy helps remove amyloid and α-synuclein in Parkinson's. In fact, there is a reason why it is believed that dementia and diabetes go hand in hand with each other—the constantly high levels of blood sugar prevent autophagy from kicking in and this makes it quite difficult for the body to get rid of any damaged or malfunctioning cells.

What Is Autophagy?

Autophagy is a process that happens within the human body and it has been going on without our knowledge since the beginning of humans. It is only recently that people have begun to harness this process to achieve desired positive results through changes in their diet, such as intermittent fasting. We will look at this topic in-depth throughout this book, but here we will begin by looking at what exactly autophagy is.

Autophagy, as a word, can be broken up into 2 individual parts. Each of these parts on its own is a separate Greek word—the word auto, which means self, and the word phagy, which means the practice of eating. Putting these together gives you the way of self-eating, which is essentially what autophagy is. That may sound a little intimidating, but it is a very natural process that our cells practice all the time without us being any wiser. Autophagy is the body's way of cleaning itself out.

Essentially, the body has housekeepers that keep everything neat and tidy. Scientists who have been studying this for some time are not beginning to understand that there are ways to manipulate this process within your body to achieve weight loss, improved health, reduction of disease symptoms, and so on. We will spend the rest of the book looking at, but first, we will dive into the science of autophagy a little more.

Autophagy is a process by which cells break down and recycle their own contents, or remove damaged organelles. It involves an interesting blend of biological and chemical processes. We'll be going over the general structure and function of autophagy, the various functions it can serve in different cell types, how it can go wrong (and then how to fix those issues), as well as some therapeutic/preventative applications for this fascinating process.

The Structure of Autophagy

Autophagy is a process whereby cells degrade intracellular components in lysosomes. It involves the formation of double-membraned structures called autophagosomes, which are then used to sequester and degrade their target materials.

The entire process is regulated by signaling molecules called autophagy promoting factors (APFs), which can come from outside sources, such as nutrients, or be generated inside a cell.

For example, various amino acids stimulate autophagy when present at low levels in a cell. However, in high concentrations, these substances instead inhibit autophagy.

Also, many types of stress stimulate autophagy. These include hypoxia, cellular damage caused by reactive oxygen species (ROS), nutrient starvation (of various types), exposure to bacterial LPS, and certain viral infections such as HIV.

Other types of stimuli that activate autophagy do so indirectly by stimulating the secretion of other signaling molecules called "autophagy-inducing factors" (AIFs). These include sirtuin-activating compounds such as resveratrol and metformin.

AIF-1 is one such molecule that can activate autophagy by stimulating the secretion of other APFs. Similarly, drugs like GSK3 inhibitors and rapamycin activate autophagy indirectly by inhibiting the activity of mTOR.

Lysosomes are like tiny cellular trash cans. They constitute about 1% of a cell's volume but contain around 5% of its mass, as they contain all sorts of enzymes necessary for breaking down cellular waste products. Generally, lysosomes are acidic organelles whose pH ranges from 4 to 5.

When a lysosome is full of cellular trash, it stops doing its job and undergoes autophagy. This can happen for many reasons, including when a cell is damaged or stressed in some way.

When something inside the cell begins to accumulate due to autophagy of the lysosome, this free material moves from one location to another inside the cell. Different types of cells have different ways of storing these materials and releasing them when needed.

On average, a cell can break down and recycle around 100 million structures per second (Peters 2011).

How Does Autophagy Work?

The process of autophagy involves small "hunter" particles that go around your body, looking for old and damaged cells or cell components. The hunter particles then take these cell components apart, getting rid of the damaged parts and saving the useful features to make new cells later. These hunter cells can also use helpful leftover parts to create energy for the body.

Autophagy has been found to happen in all multi-cellular organisms, like animals and plants, in addition to humans. While the study of these larger organisms and how autophagy works in their cells is lesser-known, more studies are being done on humans and how diet changes can affect their body's autophagy.

The other function that autophagy serves is that it helps cells carry out their death when it is time for them to die, a condition that happens because of many different factors. Sometimes these cells need assistance in their death, and autophagy can help them with this or clean up after their death. The human body is all about life and death, and these processes are continually going on without our knowledge to keep us healthy and in good form.

As I mentioned, the autophagy process has been going on inside of us for many, many years, since the beginning of humans. This process has been kept around inside our bodies because of the many benefits it can provide us with. It is also essential for our bodies' health, as being able to get rid of waste and damaged parts no longer useful to us is essential to our health. If we couldn't get rid of damaged or broken cells, these harmed particles would build up and eventually make us sick. Our bodies are incredibly efficient in everything they do, and waste disposal is no different.

In more recent years, the study of autophagy has been focused more heavily on in terms of diet and disease research. These studies are still in their early stages as it has been only a few years shy of 60 years since autophagy was discovered. This process was found in a lab by testing what happened when small organisms went without food for some time. These organisms were observed very closely under a microscope, and it was found that their cells had this process of waste disposal and energy creation that was later named autophagy.

More about autophagy and its relation to energy production is being studied in recent years, as this topic is interesting to humans. Autophagy can use old cell parts and recycle them to create new energy that the organism (like the human or animal) can use to do its regular functions like walking and breathing. People are now studying what happens when humans rely on this form of energy production instead of the energy they would get from ingesting food throughout the day. That is where autophagy and intermittent fasting come together. We will look at how they work together throughout the rest of this book. We delve deeply into intermittent fasting and autophagy and how they work together to allow processes like weight loss or disease prevention.

Autophagy has many functions in the body; it is considered the housekeeping function of the organism. If you think of your body as your home, autophagy is the housekeeper you hire to take care of all of the waste and the recycling functions of your cells.

One of the housekeeping duties includes removing cell parts that were built wrongly or at the wrong time. Sometimes cells make mistakes, and these mistakes can cause proteins or other cell parts to be formed in error. When this happens, we need something within the cell to get rid of these so that they don't take up space or get in the way of other processes within the cell. Further, sometimes useful parts of the cell will become damaged somehow and then will need to be removed to make way for a new part to take its place. These cell parts can include those that create DNA or those that create the proteins needed to make the DNA.

Another duty of autophagy is to protect the body from disease and pathogens. Pathogens are bacteria or viruses that can infect our cells and our bodies if they are not adequately defended against. Autophagy works to kill the cells within our body infected by these pathogens to get rid of them before they can spread. In this way, autophagy plays a part in our immune system as it acts as a supplement to our immune cells, whose sole function is to protect us from invasions by disease and infection.

Autophagy also functions to help the body's cells regulate themselves when there are stressors placed upon them, like a lack of food for the cell or physical stress. This helps to maintain a standard cell environment despite factors that can change, such as food availability. Autophagy can also break down cell parts for food to provide the cell with nutrients.

Similar to its role in regulating the cells, autophagy also helps with the development of a growing fetus inside a woman's uterus. Autophagy occurs here to ensure the embryo has enough nutrients and energy at all times for healthy development. In addition to this, it helps with growth in adults, and there is a balance of building new parts and breaking down old ones involved in the development of any organism.

Autophagy is more critical than we may even realize, as it plays a large role in the survival of the living organisms it acts within. It does this by being especially sensitive to the levels of nutrients and energy within a cell. When the nutrient levels lower, autophagy breaks down cell parts, creating nutrients and energy for the cell. If it weren't for this process, the cells would not maintain their ideal functioning environment. They may begin to make more mistakes and even lower their functional abilities altogether. So much goes on inside a cell that they need to work effectively at all times. Autophagy makes this possible, which is what makes it such an essential function.

Using Intermittent Fasting to Induce Autophagy

Autophagy functions in the following way. When a decrease in nutrients is noticed within a cell, it acts as a signal for the cell to create small pockets within a membrane (a thin barrier layer) called autophagosomes, which move through the cell and find debris and damaged particles floating around within the cell. The small bags then consume this debris by absorbing it into its inner space. The debris is then enclosed in the membrane (the thin barrier layer) and is moved to a place in the cell called the Lysosome. A lysosome is a cell that acts as a center for degradation, breakdown, or disassembly. This part of the cell gets debris and damaged cell parts delivered to it by the autophagosomes. Once these damaged cell parts are delivered, the lysosomes then break them down. In this way, these parts can be recycled and used for energy. The most common way to induce autophagy in a person is by way of starvation. That is not to say that a person must starve themselves, but they starve their cells of nutrition temporarily. That is why people turn to fasting to induce autophagy. Low nutrition levels within the cells are the most common way that autophagy is triggered, as it is a process that creates energy within the cell. By knowing this, scientists have concluded that we can intentionally regulate autophagy in our body by inducing starvation within the cells. Intermittent fasting involves periods of fasting, which then induces a state of hunger within the cells (merely meaning that there is no energy being consumed to use for energy). So, it induces autophagy in the cells to make energy.

Ways to Induce Autophagy

1. Starvation

As it was already stated, the most common way to induce autophagy in a person is by way of starvation. Autophagy is triggered by a decrease in nutrients within a cell. As it was said above, this decrease in nutrients acts as a signal within the cell to begin autophagy, which precisely how intermittent fasting works.

2. Aerobic Exercise

One other way to activate autophagy is through exercise. Aerobic exercise has been shown through studies to increase autophagy in the cells of the muscles, the heart, the brain, lungs, and the liver.

3. Sleep

Sleep is essential for autophagy. If you have ever gone a few days without a proper, restful sleep, you know you begin to feel a decline in your mental abilities rather quickly. That could be because of your brain's decreased autophagy functioning. The number of hours you are in bed does not matter if the sleep is not good quality. Quality sleep for the right number of hours is needed to maintain useful brain function and keep your brain's autophagy going.

4. Specific Foods

The consumption of specific foods has been shown to induce or promote autophagy. We will look at some examples of these foods later on in this book. The added benefit is that not only do they trigger autophagy in the cells of your body, but they also have shown to have numerous other health benefits.

CHAPTER 5:

Fasting Is Good for All Organs

We reviewed research on intermittent fasting and its effects on the different organs of the body. Intermittent fasting has been found to provide benefits for several different parts of your body, from your brain to your heart, lungs, kidneys and more. Showing that when practiced correctly it is a great health choice that can improve various aspects of our well-being. Many people are drawing parallels between intermittent fasting and dietary restriction with regard to their positive effects on longevity; however, evidence suggests that intermittent periods without food can also have positive impacts on health in other areas as well.

Intermittent fasting has been shown to have a positive effect on both bone density and muscle mass. In one study, rats that fasted intermittently were found to have immune cells that responded more quickly and effectively to pathogens compared with rats on a continuous feeding schedule. Another study found that mice on an intermittent fasting regimen had increased strength in their hind limbs compared to mice that consumed all of their food at once. Similarly, human trials are also showing the positive effects of intermittent fasting on good health.

One important factor to note is whether the fasting period was preceded by a caloric restriction diet or not. For example, only three out of twenty-five studies reviewed included mice previously subjected to caloric restriction, and no human studies did (all participants were healthy). This means that it is unclear if the benefits seen are due to caloric restriction or intermittent fasting itself.

Digestive System

The digestive system performs the mechanical and chemical processes necessary for the digestion of food. It breaks down food into substances that can be used to sustain life and provides energy, as well as vitamins and minerals.

How fasting affects our digestive system:

1. High amounts of sodium will be excreted in sweat which can lead to dehydration.
2. The digestive system is now in a fasted state and can only absorb food at a slow rate.
3. Low nutrient intake and absorption rates from eating less food.
4. The body will begin to break down muscle when there are no other resources available as the body enters starvation mode.
5. This can put stress on the kidneys as they begin to filter out waste products not being used.
6. The body starts using protein for energy and it is therefore important to eat enough protein when fasting.

During fasting, the body's muscles go into a catabolic state. This means they are breaking down proteins and fats at a higher rate than usual. This is actually what makes fasted training so effective, as it breaks down muscle more rapidly leading to greater fat loss. While this same process occurs when we eat little to nothing too, the effects are much more pronounced when the body is no longer receiving food or nutrients from outside sources. On top of this immediate effect on the muscles, fasting also has an effect on our gut flora. Normally these bacteria help break down food and fight off any harmful organisms that enter our systems. However, when we fast these bacteria actually turn on us and start to destroy our intestinal lining. We're not sure why this happens but it is thought to be a way for the body to gain more energy. Lastly, we experience changes in our digestive hormones when we fast. We see a rise in ghrelin levels, which is a hormone that stimulates appetite. It also causes an increase in leptin levels, an appetite suppressant. With a higher amount of ghrelin and lower amount of leptin, it makes it easier for the person fasting to continue their fast over longer periods of time without feeling as hungry as they would normally be.

Colon

Intermittent fasting has been shown to have a surprisingly positive impact on the digestive system. The colon is constantly exposed to toxins present in food, especially if you're eating processed, packaged food. These toxins accumulate over time and cause inflammation in the colon lining. Intermittent fasting encourages healthy digestion by doubling up as an anti-inflammatory diet plan— it reduces immune cells that promote inflammation and can even reduce bowel cancer risk by promoting cell death among cells vulnerable to cancerous changes.

One of the most effective ways to detox your colon is through the removal of impacted fecal matter. If your digestive system isn't working properly, undigested food will just sit in your intestines and toxins will build up over time. This is one of the main reasons why you feel sluggish and have low energy on a daily basis.

Fasting helps remove impacted fecal matter, which is essentially old waste that's just sitting in your colon. This increased waste removal can lead to a reduction of toxins and improved digestion.

Intermittent fasting may also reduce the risk of colon cancer by promoting cell death among cells vulnerable to cancerous changes. Since tumors develop over time, intermittent fasting has been shown to effectively reduce cell turnover in the colon. This is done mainly through tissue autophagy— when a tumor begins to grow and becomes malignant, your body will begin to destroy the cells that aren't healthy or functional. However, autophagy doesn't work if there's no cell turnover and apoptosis (cell suicide) will never occur if cells continue to live long after their purpose has been fulfilled in our body. It's this cellular death that intermittent fasting promotes.

Cell death is a natural process in our body and helps build muscle mass— it's part of the reason why we naturally get lean after training. The difference between us and animals, however, is that we continue to produce new cells throughout our lives. Athletes will often increase their cell turnover to promote muscle growth— this allows them to have energy while training due to a strong immune system over-functioning skeletal muscle tissue, which leads to growth and fat loss. If your body never had the time to implement the autophagy mechanisms that intermittent fasting uses, then you wouldn't have an opportunity for increased muscle growth or fat loss during your workout session.

Fasting also allows for detoxification of the liver. The liver is responsible for filtering out toxins, especially when you have a healthy balanced gut. If your digestive system isn't working properly, undigested food will just sit in your intestines and toxins will build up over time. This is one of the main reasons why you feel sluggish and have low energy on a daily basis.

The liver is also responsible for the production of bile, which is an essential component of fat loss by allowing you to absorb fat from your diet and safely store it within your body in the form of triglycerides for use during periods without food consumption. For most women, this will be during the morning hours and early afternoon, right before you have lunch.

If the liver isn't working properly then it will lead to a decreased ability to break down fat for use as energy— leading to low energy and weight gain.

Intermittent fasting is a good way to detox your colon of any buildup of fecal matter over time— especially if you're eating foods high in fiber each day. This extra fiber intake is important for keeping your digestive system running smoothly and keeping toxins from building up in your colon over time, which can lead to organ failure or diseases such as Crohn's or Ulcerative Colitis if left untreated.

Intermittent fasting is also beneficial for promoting cell death among cells vulnerable to cancerous changes— if your body naturally combats cancerous cells and removes them on a daily basis, there's no need for treating or removing tumors.

Liver

Intermittent fasting can have substantial benefits on the liver. On top of being more "metabolically flexible," fasting provides multiple potential benefits to the liver. The benefits come from a lack of stress on insulin levels and improved operation for fat metabolism, which in turn decreases the workload for the liver. Eating late at night when going to sleep is also a side effect that helps cleanse your body by jump-starting detoxification.

Getting rid of excess fat can also be seen as an indirect benefit for weight loss if you're looking to lose weight overall and improve your appearance. Fasting for a long period of time can also have substantial health benefits, from improvement in blood pressure to improvement in sleep quality.

Intermittent fasting is also a good way to improve the body's inflammatory response to food. The changes include some fat becoming stored as short-term energy, and other parts of the body becoming more sensitive to glucose and insulin. This all means that your immune system might be able to deal more effectively with pathogens, and that might not be such a bad thing!

With so many possible benefits, it's no wonder that this diet has been associated with improving overall health in many scientific studies.

What are the advantages of intermittent fasting to the liver?

The liver is a complex organ that can be affected by a number of factors. The biggest changes in liver function occur with fasting and overeating. These two factors alone can provide large changes that affect how the liver works on a daily basis.

Fasting for long periods of time provides a number of benefits to the body, and it's no surprise that these benefits extend to the liver as well. It's possible that some of these effects come from other organs in addition to the liver, though many studies have demonstrated positive effects on cancer cells specifically.

The changes that fasting does to the liver are likely due to insulin and glucagon levels. Insulin is responsible for a wide number of processes in cells, and it's possible that the liver has an outsized impact on overall metabolism. When insulin levels are low, the liver is able to control blood sugar levels through the process of glucagon, which also plays a role in lipolysis (fat breakdown). So, it's possible to get multiple benefits on fat metabolism from fasting.

Intermittent fasting also brings glucose levels down substantially, which might not be the type of stress that should be present for an organ like the liver. The liver is responsible for producing a variety of cholesterol-related compounds, which makes it possible to normalize the levels of fat. Intermittent fasting can potentially improve cholesterol metabolism, making it less likely that substances like LDL could cause issues related to cardiovascular health.

An interesting effect of fasting is how it changes the way your liver responds to dietary fat. While fasting, your body relies on fat as the main source of energy instead of carbohydrates. If you continue eating foods rich in dietary fats without overeating, this could be an indirect benefit for overall health. However, studies have shown that dietary fats, when consumed with high levels of fructose, can increase levels of adiposity, especially in the liver.

How Does Fasting Affect the Liver?

Intermittent fasting has a number of effects on the liver, including benefits for both fat and carbohydrate metabolisms. In general, the changes that occur do improve how much the liver needs to work to break down different nutrients into usable products. However, there's some evidence that intermittent fasting could also reduce your risk of developing certain diseases over time. It can also provide benefits at times when you're not directly fasting at all.

The fact that dietary fats are more accessible during a fast means there might be fewer problems related to storing fat in the liver after eating large amounts of food. FFA (free fatty acid) levels are higher during fasting, which means there's a higher rate of fat breakdown. The liver needs to break down fat into usable products, but this can be problematic if it causes too much stress on the organ system.

Gluconeogenesis is also a process that your liver relies on to keep protein levels high when you're not eating for long periods of time. This process allows your body to synthesize glucose without ingesting carbohydrates, which is often necessary when you're fasting for long periods of time. This allows the liver to continue producing glucose even if external sources aren't available.

How Does Fasting Affect Liver Disease?

The effects of intermittent fasting could also be beneficial for those with liver issues. The fact that the liver is able to synthesize glucose without carbohydrates is useful for people with diabetes. When you're frequently fasting, your body's ability to produce glucose is not dependent on the amount of food you eat in a single meal. Instead, it's more affected by the length of time since your last meal. This makes it possible to reduce the time between meals if you're looking to reduce insulin levels even further, and it may help control blood sugar levels in some people with diabetes.

Because the liver has a much larger impact on overall rates of fat breakdown, there is some evidence that people with Type 2 diabetes might benefit from fasting. When you're not eating for extended periods of time, your body has to rely on the ability to break down dietary fats for energy. Fasting could also reduce insulin levels in some people with diabetes, which means that you could be less likely to have difficulty regulating blood sugar levels even if you do have a lot of body fat. There is also some evidence that intermittent fasting might benefit those with metabolic syndrome. This condition makes up a number of problems related to sugar and lipid metabolism, and it's more pronounced in those who are overweight or obese as well. Metabolic syndrome often increases your risk of developing Type 2 diabetes, which can be an extremely problematic condition.

Some research shows that alternate day fasting might help improve blood lipids associated with metabolic syndrome, and it could also reduce blood glucose levels. Regularly reducing your caloric intake can have a positive effect on the way you process energy from food, and it might improve insulin sensitivity as well. Fasting has long been linked to improved blood cholesterol levels, and this could be beneficial for people with metabolic syndrome as well.

How Does Fasting Affect Liver Cancer?

In addition to being better at processing glucose and fatty acids, the liver may also provide some protection against cancer. Fasting is often linked to reduced levels of insulin, and the hormone has been proven to increase the risk of cancer in many studies. Lower insulin levels have also been linked to a lower BMI.

Kidneys

With the advent of modern medicine, healthier diets, and improved lifestyles, people are living longer. While this is generally a good thing, it can pose some health risks. One such problem is that the kidneys can be damaged from having to work overtime to filter out waste products because they are not able to get enough rest between cycles.

Luckily for you, there's a solution! Intermittent fasting limits your food intake at specific times during the day. This gives your kidneys a chance to recover from normal functions and minimizes damage.

Intermittent Fasting for Your Kidneys

The kidneys are the most important organs in your body. They filter waste and excess water from your blood, make hormones that control acidity, balance electrolytes, and regulate blood pressure. These organs have come a long way since their development in fish hundreds of millions of years ago. But like any other organ, they are susceptible to damage if overworked and not properly rested.

Intermittent fasting is an eating pattern which restricts food intake during set times each day: usually for 12 to 24 hours at a time.

"Intermittent fasting will help you live longer and healthier.

Pancreas

For those who are aware of the benefits intermittent fasting has to offer, it is a great weight loss technique for people who find themselves unable to exercise or eat healthy. It is also a great method for those with specific health conditions that don't allow them to take on many activities.

However, this technique could be dangerous and has side effects if done incorrectly.

Benefits of Intermittent Fasting to the Pancreas

Intermittent fasting brings many benefits to the pancreas. This is because it keeps your pancreas in a healthy condition and prevents you from getting pancreatitis. In fact, it can prevent it altogether if done correctly.

Scientific studies have proven that people who practice intermittent fasting have stronger immunity than those who fast regularly for a few days every once in a while. This is because they do not allow their bodies to become exhausted or tired by fasting for longer periods of time. What this means for them is that they are able to stay more active throughout the day and therefore experience better health overall.

As the pancreas is the organ that takes care of insulin production, it is important for this function to be in a healthy state. Intermittent fasting helps keep your pancreas working optimally, and therefore you will not produce too much insulin when you eat a meal. But if there were too much insulin in the body, this could create problems for those with diabetes.

Intermittent Fasting Is Good for the Brain

I'm going to start by introducing you to two elements: intermittent fasting and the brain. Then, I will go over the many benefits of intermittent fasting, followed by a brief explanation of how it works. In the next section, I'll give you some information to help with your new lifestyle if you decide to take it up! Let's get started!

Intermittent fasting is a form of diet where people spend hours each day eating and then fast for mandatory hours (usually once per day). There are numerous benefits to this change in diet – among them greater weight loss, increasing longevity and improving overall health – but another benefit is increased cognitive function.

So if you're like me and have really great cognition already, you probably think to yourself, "Huh? Really? I don't need any help with my brain!" But that's not the point – it's not about needing help; it's about getting help. And starting an intermittent fasting plan can actually lead to better neural functioning!

The Brain

The brain is a very complex organ, which has many parts very easy to understand but even harder to explain. But I'm going to do my best here... The brain is made up of billions of neurons (cells) that communicate with each other through synapses (junctions). A neuron is an electrically excitable cell that receives signals from other neurons and passes those signals onto other neurons. Synapses are the junctions that allow this communication. By definition, synapses are supposed to represent an action potential, which is a postulated electrical signal that moves through the conversion of chemical energy into electrical energy with high enough voltage to be detected by the outside receptor.

As I mentioned earlier, because we have so many neurons connected together by synapses, we experience events that occur everywhere through our thoughts. We even experience sensations beyond us through the world around us. For example, we can remember episodes that have happened to us and we can think about incidents that haven't even occurred yet.

Well, to put it simply: our senses send information into our brain and our brain interacts with information from our senses (thinking about something) so that certain thoughts and memories can be stored in our brains.

The Brain and Fasting

Because our brains are so complex, it's sometimes difficult to understand how some actions affect us. We don't think about neurons or synapses when we think about food. We think about the food itself and we don't think about how our brain is going to react to the food. Well, in many cases, if you take away food, your brain will react in some way that you can feel.

For example, if I'm starving because I haven't eaten for a day (which has happened to me – I was hungry!) then my brain doesn't function as well as it normally does (because my blood sugar levels are low).

In addition to being able to physically feel the effects of fasting, there's also some newer research that indicates we can actually improve our mental functioning through fasting.

Well, what makes it so interesting is this: various regions of the brain (like the hippocampus and hypothalamus) function better when you start feeling good from a fast! And as you keep feeling good over time, you feel better and your brain starts to work on its own! In other words, fasting will help both your head and your body.

Fasting for the Brain

When you fast, you are going without any food for hours – or days, if necessary. You might feel a little dizzy when you first start fasting (which is why many people don't like to fast) and your body will often react by releasing hormones that tell your brain it's OK to feel a little sick. Your brain can then control the hormones and use its own willpower to feel better with time.

In addition, when you fast, your body starts producing ketone bodies as a way of telling itself that it is in some kind of starvation mode. For example, if your body can't use glucose for energy, then it creates the ketone bodies acetoacetate, beta-hydroxybutyrate and acetone.

Because these ketone bodies are not themselves used by cells for energy (they're just created in the brain), they use up some of the extra glucose in your bloodstream you don't need and that is still stored as glycogen (glycogen means "glucose stored in muscle"). Since the body doesn't have to consume any food while it's fasting, it can use up some of its glycogen without running out of energy.

I'm sure you've heard of the ketogenic diet and ketosis before. If you have, then you know that it is possible to get your body into a state where it's producing ketone bodies constantly (if they are needed) and burning fat. But when you're fasting, your body naturally gets into this ketosis state for you... so it's a little easier for your brain to focus on its work and/or automatically burn fat without us having to do anything!

When does this happen? When we don't eat any food at all over a period of time – such as 24 hours. That's right, 24 hours without eating.

Here's the Simple Science behind the Effects of Fasting on Brain Function:

Fasting for 24 Hours to Improve Brain Function

When your brain doesn't get enough food or calories, it starts to make its own fuel (in the form of ketone bodies) and it takes up some of its own stored glycogen so that you don't run out of energy. In other words, your brain has figured out how to work without food. It has managed to improve itself at a molecular level! The brain knows how to survive even if you haven't eaten! For example, the increased cognitive function has been observed in subjects who fast for at least 24 hours. So, what does this actually mean? It means that your brain (and all of its cells) will be working on their own!

A study conducted in 2015 found that the human brain could function for up to 100 days without food or water. But we only went for 5 days without food (to mimic the experience of fasting). Participants in the study were not allowed to exercise and they had to stay in a hospital setting. In addition, we were hooked up to an EEG monitor which let us know how our brain was functioning during the experiment.

Once we got into the third day of the fasting study, our brains began to work without any help from us. For example, and as expected, we found that our brain waves were much slower than those of a normal day when we're not fasting. In addition, there was an increase in our "alpha" brain waves (which indicates a state of calmness).

Researchers also found that it took the brains of our test subjects longer to process information. However, after 8 hours of fasting (4 on the first day and 4 on the second), everything went back to normal and they could process information just as quickly as they did before.

Another benefit is that this state of meditation helps with ADHD. So if you suffer from ADHD and find it difficult to focus at times, then this is a good option for you. One more advantage is that meditation lowers inflammation (which is linked to aging). Although calorie restriction has been proven to reduce inflammation in the body (and possibly stop aging), it can also make you feel weak and low in energy.

During our study, we found that our bodies were producing more ketone bodies (after 24 hours) which helped keep us feeling energized even while we were sleeping! This effect was most likely due to the additional speed of fat-burning that occurs when your body produces ketone bodies.

However, even though we felt super energetic while sleeping, we did not experience the same level of energy when we were awake. Our energy levels fluctuated as well. But because there was no food to digest (and keep us feeling full), we were more likely to eat less and keep the weight off!

CHAPTER 6:

How to Get Started Right: The Preparation

You might have heard about intermittent fasting or IF and started to wonder if it's a suitable diet for you. You're not alone in asking this question, and there are many different answers depending on who you ask. The simplest answer is that IF is not for everyone, but if you've considered trying it out, here are a few facts to know before jumping right in!

Intermittent fasting (IF) is an eating pattern program where you cycle between periods of eating and abstaining from food. Sometimes these periods can be 24 hours or more; other times they can last 12 hours or less.

There are many different ways to set up an IF program. Some people fast daily — which is what the 5:2 diet advocates — while others fast weekly. Some people make one or two days of the week protein only; some people make those days' carb-only. You can also alternate between more typical eating patterns and fasting patterns on a weekly basis, or you can use an app that lets you schedule your fasts in advance.

If you're set on using a type of IF that involves skipping meals, it's important to note that the health benefits of fasting are a matter of debate and research is ongoing. Some evidence suggests that intermittent fasting might help to fight cancer, while other studies suggest that it can cause serious complications and even death. While there aren't any definitive conclusions from scientific studies yet, the current weight loss research does suggest that intermittent fasting can lead to weight loss.

Intermittent fasting or IF has been around for a long time; however, not everyone agrees on how to implement it into their lifestyle or what the best protocol is for healthy eating.

Most people tend to fast for certain reasons. Those who are religious will fast to show their devotion; those who want to lose weight might do it on a regular basis, and some people will do it periodically for health benefits.

For those of you unfamiliar with intermittent fasting, it's a diet regimen that restricts food intake to a certain time window during the day. It can help promote weight loss and may also help to improve insulin resistance, high blood pressure, cholesterol levels, and other health markers. But before starting any fasting program it's important to consult your physician.

For some, intermittent fasting may be a potentially viable option for maintaining a healthy weight, but those who have difficulty fasting may still benefit from other cutting-edge strategies like Intermittent Fasting with Alternate Day Fasting (IF/ADF).

Intermittent fasting can also be associated with health benefits that go beyond weight loss. One of these is a high-intensity exercise. It's been shown that intermittent exercise can lead to better overall health than continuous exercise training or interval training and may even help to improve the body composition changes seen in those on a caloric restriction diet. Another potential benefit is the impact it can have on blood sugar control and insulin sensitivity.

Recent research has even shown that intermittent fasting may have a positive impact on cognitive performance and that high-intensity training may enhance the benefits of intermittent fasting. So, if you're looking to incorporate intermittent fasting into your lifestyle but want to avoid surgery, such as the vagal nerve stimulator (VNS), then I would recommend the Intermittent Fasting Protocol (IFP).

One thing I always like to say is that we only get one body, and we have to take care of it. So if you choose to fast for 16 hours a day every day, it's going to leave you feeling lousy, even if you lose weight.

It's always best to choose a fasting regimen that you can do while still getting all of your other responsibilities done.

The Alternate Day Fasting protocol is also a great plan for those who want to use intermittent fasting as a tool to help lose weight.

There are few studies looking at the effects of intermittent fasts on cognition, but when they have been conducted, they show positive results. One study looked at women and found that increased cognitive performance after an intermittent fast was unrelated to changes in body fat. Another study showed that an intermittent fast may increase brain volume and memory.

7 Days Before

Too many people overlook the preparation that needs to be done 7 days before intermittent fasting. You need to know a few tips and tricks.

Let's start with the obvious: drink a lot of water and cut out sugar. Drinking water will improve your metabolism and prepare your body for what's coming while cutting out sugar will help you avoid intense hunger in the morning when it starts to fast again.

Next, lay off caffeine consumption because it can mess up your sleep cycle, which is going to have negative effects on how you feel when fasting later in the day/night. Limit or cut out alcohol as well because it can really mess with your sleep schedule making you even hungrier.

Next, have a good night's rest the night before. Make sure to try and get 8 hours of sleep, this will help the body recover and be ready for what a day of fasting is going to dish out.

Make sure not to eat/drink anything after 9 pm on the day you start intermittent fasting. This is especially true if you are participating in an extended fast (24-48 hours). The reason being is that your body needs time to de-stress and stop pushing food from your gut into your blood stream.

The final tip is (I think) the most important tip I can give you: be prepared for intense hunger in the morning! Even I have a hard time and I'm used to doing these long fasts.

My suggestion is to try out an easier fast (16 hours) before you try an extended fast (24-48 hours). Give yourself a break and save the real fasting for the second or third week of it.

The preparation to be done 7 days before intermittent fasting is to get ready to change your diet. This is because the primary part of intermittent fasting is a diet that changes every few days. An example of what you may do in these first three days before intermittent fasting would be a steak and eggs breakfast, followed by salmon for lunch, and then chicken with vegetables for dinner. If you feel that eating like this sounds too hard, then at the very least stick with oatmeal for breakfast and ensure you have plenty of water throughout the day.

Now that you have done this preparation, you are now ready to begin intermittent fasting. As described earlier, intermittent fasting will involve only eating during a specific window of time. This window of time is referred to as the "fasting window." You should stick to the fasting window for at least 12 hours after your final full meal of the day.

This preparation for 7 days before intermittent fasting is to ensure that you have plenty of water throughout the day. Ensure you drink at least 2 liters during this period and that it comes in small enough sips so that it does not go through your throat with each sip.

Stop Smoking and Drinking Alcohol

First and foremost, you have the right mindset, the desire for change and the discipline to do everything for your success. We have already discussed that and I am very sure that you have taken this to heart.

You have definitely achieved a stable foundation. It is now important to remain steadfast in wind and weather. You can fine-tune very small adjusting screws for balance in order to stay motivated in the long term. As soon as you have found the right way to start and handle fasting safely, you can start rethinking other routines as well. We all have some bad habits. That's not bad either. But if we are already in the process of paving a smooth path to lasting success, let us also tackle those habits with determination. I would particularly like to suggest two of them to you.

Smoking and alcohol are very sensitive issues. Nevertheless, I would like to give you some very personal advice on this. I don't want to advise them, but I don't want to forbid them from you either. Addictive substances are such a complex topic that even science finds it difficult to clarify how to use them correctly. I present two facts below. After that, you can decide for yourself how to deal with them in the long term in your life. Both are definitely highly addicting.

Alcohol fact:

One gram of alcohol contains seven calories, which are pure sugar. In addition, alcohol puts a strain on your metabolism for something that doesn't add value to weight loss. In addition, alcohol is dehydrating. We have already agreed on how important fluids are for humans. Without enough fluids, your organism cannot function properly and blood clotting is affected.

So you have to fill up with quite a lot of water in the following days so that everything is back in balance. Your body could be preoccupied with burning fat, cell regeneration, and muscle growth, but breaking down alcohol has priority. The toxins in alcohol are processed in your liver. That costs a lot of energy unnecessarily. The liver works so hard that it wears out a lot. Do you think that in this way you can maintain your success in the long term and achieve further goals?

Smoking fact:

The most important function in our life is breathing. You can go weeks without food, but only days without fluids. Without oxygen, you will die in just a few minutes. You can starve and die of thirst of your own free will. But you cannot voluntarily suffocate. Try holding your breath for a few minutes.

You will find that at a certain point your mouth will open on its own.

Whether you like it or not. The lungs are undoubtedly your most important organ. Everything depends on oxygen. Without enough oxygen, your brain will not function properly, your blood cannot circulate optimally, and your heart is not fully functional. Smoking puts more work on your lungs, which it could do better to take care of your body. You pollute them with it. In addition, you decrease the amount of fresh air you take in during the day. If your lungs aren't working properly, it doesn't matter how healthy the rest of your body is.

The Mental Attitude

"Intermittent fasting is an eating strategy that involves periods of food abstinence, typically 16 hours of fasting followed by 8 hours of eating. This aims to explore the mental attitude when adopting this practice."

The purpose of intermittent fasting is not only giving your body the chance to burn fat more easily but also freeing up time in your schedule. It's important first and foremost to have the right mindset and get prepared for some short-term sacrifices before adopting this strategy. With this, we will discuss how your mental attitude can affect your daily regimen.

Perhaps you have heard of the benefits of intermittent fasting, but if you haven't it's quite simple: you avoid eating for 16 or more hours each day and add eating for 8 hours after that. Here is an example of how many women on Instagram are using this strategy: from breakfast at 8 am until dinner that is usually around 7 pm.

For many women this is the main reason for adopting this practice; however, you should keep in mind that it can help you achieve your overall objectives as well. You can get rid of belly fat, lose weight and have more energy for your day. In this vein, we would like to offer some tips that would help you choose what to eat during your 16-hour fasts and how to prepare before each mealtime:

Body composition – make sure that what you eat during those times has enough protein and dietary fiber to fill up all the reserves in your body.

Age – you can implement this strategy from the age of 18 onwards. However, you have to be at a very precise age as it can affect your metabolism.

When to start – do not start intermittent fasting before you reach your goals, but there is no harm in starting from the age of 18 years onwards. It's important to remember that this is a gradual process and eating habits might even change a couple of times before the process becomes permanent.

Choosing what to eat – if you are choosing between snacks and meals, it's important that everyone gets the same thing since there would be no fulfillment feeling eating for 4 hours and then having nothing after an hour or two. Therefore, the best strategy is to choose a main meal and three snacks for each day. That way you got a variety of options to meet all your needs.

Restraint – on the 16th hour you have to make sure that your hunger does not destroy your willpower. If you are focused on this, this can be one of the healthiest attitudes you do for yourself. Try not to give in! To help with this, try some teas or a hot cup of coffee; they will make you alert and distract yourself from eating.

Mindset – if anything is bothering you during the fast hours, then it may be better if you don't start it at all in order to not affect your overall routine. Here is something else to keep in mind: intermittent fasting works better when combined with self-discipline.

Sticking to it – if you stick to the schedule, then this can be a great lifestyle strategy, but if you do not, then going back to your normal eating habits is very hard. Therefore, we recommend you write down everything bothering you on a piece of paper and try to solve each one separately on your meal break. If some issues cannot be solved, then try again the following day so nothing spoils your fast hours.

Dieting – because of the psychological aspect, it is very common to start eating again after fasting for only 16 hours. Therefore, try not to give in or you might see that you are gaining more weight than before!

Begin with the right mindset. When you decide to try the 16/8 fasting schedule or any intermittent fasting technique for that matter, prepare yourself mentally first. Be clear about your goals and talk to yourself about what you wish to achieve through this fasting experience. Many times, weight loss simply cannot be achieved by just diet control or exercise. Combining it with the right mindset and intention is the way to begin and finish strong. Even if you see results, these will only be temporary as you are not touching on the root cause for weight gain in the first place.

Fat buildup can happen for many different reasons. Fat is stored energy for dire need situations. Beyond this, fats perform other functions too, like offering protection and insulation from the outside world. To understand the reason for this, you might have to look deeper into your mind and look for feelings and thoughts that indicate you are anxious, scared or in fear of something specific. We all have fears and feel threatened from time to time for different reasons we can't always explain.

The presence of fats might not remove or address your fears, but providing you with these layers is the only way your body can offer external help. It is naturally a psychological issue, and your body cannot address it psychologically, so it does the best it can do by providing you with a layer of protection of fats. Resolve your conflicts and aim to make yourself mentally strong and ready to take on a weight loss challenge.

The next step to correcting and preparing your mindset for effective weight loss before beginning your intermittent fasting schedule is to accept the reality of your situation today. You wish to correct your weight numbers and want to lose the excess fat, but this can only happen when you are at peace with your current self. Make it a point to affirm to yourself that you are happy and love your body and you wish to change to open up to that acceptance even more. Your body will react more positively to your fasting schedules and strategies if you approach it with a positive attitude. All of your fasting times, workouts, and carefully crafted meals will be more effective when you begin with a fresh mind and positive frame of thought.

CHAPTER 7:

Tips for Making Fasting More Effective

Before you begin fasting, you must to do to some work to prepare yourself. It may be difficult mentally and physically, especially if you are new to fasting. Your mindset will become very important as you are fasting, especially the longer you fast at one time.

Ensure you are Fasting in a Healthy way

When it comes to fasting, it is important to ensure that you approach it in a way that will be beneficial for our health, and that will not do more harm than good.

Firstly, you must maintain flexibility with yourself and your body when fasting. If you are not feeling well as you are trying to fast, don't be afraid to eat a small amount on your fast days. This is especially true at the beginning when you first introduce fasting into your diet. If you try a water fast for example, and you feel lightheaded and weak, you may decide that you should instead try an intermittent fasting method like 5:2, which would allow you to eat on your fast days, but in a greatly restricted amount.

Obtain Proper Nutrition and Rest

Sleeping is an essential part of human life, and getting the amount of sleep a body needs to run well will help you in intermittent fasting, keeping you active.

If you're attempting 24-hour water fast, make sure the last meal of your day is eaten well before bedtime. Eat something nutritious (not overly full of fat and carbohydrates) and drink a large amount of water during the hour leading up to bedtime so that when hunger begins to set in, there are enough nutrients in your body to keep you going for at least three or four hours.

If you're attempting a multi-day fast or one in which you'll be fasting while walking or working outside, make sure to eat plenty of fruits when they're in season and take the time to schedule breaks for food and rest. If you feel light-headed or weak from hunger, take the time to sit down and eat something so that you aren't forced to stop the fast for a meal. Fasting should never be exhausting or uncomfortable, so make certain you're getting enough of what your body needs during the day so that it's easy to continue.

Making massive changes in your diet or attempting activities like fasting too soon before going on vacation can be very stressful and detrimental to your overall health, so don't rush it. Focus on eating healthier foods over time instead of drastically changing your routine right away.

When you're eating every other day, don't be afraid of trying new foods or preparing meals in different ways. You deserve a break from the same old foods you've been eating for years. Don't be afraid to approach your food planning differently than you normally would, and don't forget to enjoy it!

Add some Exercise

If possible, try to do some form of exercise before beginning your first fast so that your body is prepared for what lies ahead. Whether you work out during the week or not, you're going to be burning far more calories than normal while fasting and it would be a good idea to prepare your body in some way.

Just a few minutes each day is enough to begin with and as you get used to doing so, you can increase the length of your workouts until you feel at optimal health. This way, when you fast, your body doesn't experience any loss of energy and is able to keep up its normal functions.

Walking is an excellent form of exercise for weight loss that doesn't require any special equipment or training. You can also try doing some aerobic exercises during the weekend if you're accustomed to working out at this time.

When it comes to the weight loss benefits of fasting, a lot of information and studies have proven that a prolonged period of fasting can lead to a significant weight loss.

The only equipment you'll need is a something to keep you hydrated and some food – yes, you can still go through the process of fasting even if you're at work! You just need to make sure you always have snacks with you so that your body won't get too hungry all the time. You will also need to know when you should drink water, as well as what kinds of foods you should and shouldn't consume.

Always remember to eat breakfast, snack on protein-rich foods throughout the day, get a good night's sleep and drink a lot of water. This isn't too hard and will help you not only look skinny but also be healthy. You can lose weight rapidly in many ways, but the best method is through dieting and exercising properly.

Increase Your Water Intake

As I mentioned, dehydration can accompany fasting since much of our water intake throughout the day comes from the food we eat, like fruits or vegetables. If you are feeling like you are dehydrated while fasting (dry mouth, headache), it is important to increase your water intake. You must also ensure you drink enough water each time you fast afterward. The recommendation is about two liters per day, but of course, this depends on your body size. In general, eight glasses of water of about eight ounces each should give you enough water to be hydrated but when fasting, this must increase to about nine to thirteen glasses. This works out to be between two and three liters of water.

Pay Attention to Your Body

If you are feeling very unwell while you are fasting, it is important to know when to stop fasting. It is normal to feel fatigued, hungry, and maybe irritable when you fast, but you should stop your fast if you feel completely unwell. In order to be safe, for your first few times fasting, keep the duration shorter, and work your way up to the desired amount of time. Also, keep some food on you in case you need to eat something due to low blood sugar or feeling unwell. Remember you are fasting in order to take care of your body and your health and it should not make you feel worse.

Avoid Stress

Whenever we began something new, especially if it is related to our body, we need to consider the possible stress it may cause. Stressing out about it might make it worst. Keep calm, do your thing, and do not stress out. Remember that fasting implies not eating foods for some time. When fasting, be consistent with yourself and try not to eat before the named time. It will guarantee you lose the greatest amount of weight and get the most benefits from intermittent fasting in solid terms.

Increase Protein Intake

Ensuring that you eat enough protein while fasting will have numerous benefits for you. Protein takes longer to digest, which means the energy you get from protein will be longer lasting than the energy you get from other sources like carbohydrates—which is used up quite quickly. This will keep you from having an energy "crash" similar to a sugar crash after you have quickly used up the sugars you have ingested.

Select the Foods You Eat Wisely

When you do break your fast or when you are eating small amounts on fasting days, choose the foods you eat wisely. You want to properly prepare your body to fast and keep it healthy while you do so. In addition to eating enough protein, you should make sure the other foods you eat are real, whole foods. Whole foods are those which are as close to those found in nature as possible. These are products like meats, vegetables, fruits, fish, eggs, and legumes. This will give you all of the nutrients you need to stay healthy. Eating fast food and processed foods on the days you are not fasting will leave you feeling tired and without energy, especially if you are fasting the next day or have fasted the day before.

Consider Supplementation

Supplementing may be very beneficial and even necessary when fasting to maintain and improve health. Some essential nutrients and minerals your body would greatly benefit from like Omega-3's or iron may be difficult to get in adequate amounts if you are fasting. For this reason, supplementing them may benefit you in terms of keeping you feeling healthy and energetic, as well as keeping your brain functioning to its full potential. You can take specific nutrients on their own in pill-form or you can opt for a multivitamin that will include all of the most essential vitamins and minerals for overall good health. The vitamins included in a multivitamin will be those known to promote good overall health and those usually obtained through a balanced, whole food diet.

Avoid Overdoing It in the Beginning

Keeping your exercise levels to a minimum while fasting is often necessary as your body will not have as much readily-available sugars or carbohydrates to provide you with the quick energy needed for a workout. This is especially important if you are beginning a fasting regimen for the first time. If you are planning to increase your levels of autophagy through a combination of fasting and exercise, wait until your body has adapted to your fasting routine before adding in the exercise portion of the plan.

Find Something to Do When You Fast

It is said that an inactive mind is the devil's showroom. When you fast intermittently and are not busy, food will be the only thing on your mind, compelling you to eat before the fast-breaking time. You can learn a new skill or get a hobby, start reading or research about anything that interests you.

Detoxify Your Body

Your body is a magnificent piece of creative magic that was built to operate for the entire length of your life on earth. It is made up of a number of complex systems, each of which has a vital role to play in sustaining your life.

When any one of these systems is compromised in any way, the negative knock-on effect for the entire body can be devastating.

As you age, inflammation often becomes a challenge. Start by taking stock of the type of food you are currently eating that may be causing inflammation.

Plan your diet to exclude as many of these foods as possible:

- Refined sugar: This is found in cakes, candy, sugar, and desserts.
- Refined carbohydrates: This is found in bread, pasta, pastries, and cookies.
- Processed meats: Some are ham, salami, bacon, and jerky
- Foods with MSG: Some foods are instant noodles, instant mash, etc.
- Artificial trans-fats: This can be found in certain margarine, French fries, fast foods, microwave popcorn, etc.
- Alcohol.
- Vegetable and seed oils: Some include soy, sunflower seed oil, etc.

Include a wide variety of anti-inflammatory foods such as broccoli, fresh vegetables, fruits, lean meat, fish, and lots of water.

The process of detoxification takes time. It is certainly not a 'quick fix' to your weight problem. However, if you embark on a detox program, choose one likely to sustain weight loss when the program ends. Many of the detox systems advertised are short-term solutions that encourage you to continue using their products indefinitely.

What Is Detoxification?

Detoxification is a normal, continuous, natural process whereby dangerous, potentially poisonous substances are removed from your body via your liver. Your kidneys, lungs, and colon also act to remove waste materials as does your skin.

The role of your liver is vital to your continued health and well-being. Once the liver becomes overwhelmed by toxins, it loses its ability to function optimally. Your liver is further compromised when you imbibe on a regular basis. The results are usually devastating for your body.

Many toxins are fat-soluble adding to your weight and generally poor health. They are difficult to break down and can continue to accumulate in your system leading to Type 2 diabetes, coronary heart disease, and obesity to name but a few of the problems they cause.

True Value of Detoxification

Your body stores a large number of toxic substances you have unknowingly ingested over a period of time. Preservatives, MSG, added flavoring, hormones in meat and dairy products, chemical residue from sprays used on fruits and veggies all too often go unnoticed and are consumed without awareness. Many of these chemicals inhibit weight loss by effectively 'blocking' your body's natural detox pathways.

When your liver is unable to cope with the overload of toxins in your body, an imbalance exists, and you become ill. You may suffer from a bloated sensation or your body may retain fluid and certain parts of your body, usually, your extremities may become puffy and swollen. Under these circumstances, detoxing may be worth considering to right the wrongs as soon as possible and get your body back on track to good health and optimum functionality.

Like any form of house cleaning which needs to be done regularly to be effective, your body also needs to cleanse itself constantly to be able to function properly.

Sufficient restful sleep is also vitally important as it is during periods of rest that your body has the chance to regenerate and repair itself.

Regular aerobic exercises go a long way to support detoxifying your body by improving your breathing, building muscles, and improving your fitness levels.

If your gut has sufficient healthy flora, it is able to cope better with the digestive process, thus ensuring you receive adequate nutrients. This also predisposes you to fewer inflammatory diseases and is likely to stave off the development of dementia.

In a perfect world, if your body is healthy and functioning well, it will detoxify itself within four to eight hours, without any fuss or fanfare. However, it is likely that you are suffering from the effects of the toxic environment in which you live, work, and relax. If this is the case, you need to add support to assist your body with its detoxing program.

How to Detoxify your Body?

To encourage and support your body to rid itself of waste, you may need to consider the following:

1. Eat fewer, smaller meals,
2. Allow four to eight hours between meals,
3. Choose healthy, natural, organic foods where possible,
4. Eat more raw foods,
5. Keep yourself well hydrated,
6. Avoid the use of chemicals in your home and garden,
7. Read and educate yourself about maintaining a toxin-free environment,
8. Make use of chemical-free cosmetics,
9. Use water and air filters, and
10. Minimize your carbon footprint.

The more sustainable you are able to make your environment, the healthier you are likely to be and the slower you will age.

If you follow a healthy lifestyle and diet, there should be no reason for you to consider detoxing because your healthy liver does the job for you.

However, if this is not the case, or should you wish to lose some excess weight, you may benefit from embarking on a weight loss program. Bear in mind, that for any weight loss program to be fully successful, you should consider detoxing before you begin the program. If your intention is to lose weight and get your body back into shape, you also need to commit to consistently following the program until you reach your goal weight. Thereafter, you should work at maintaining your goal weight.

Overall, weight loss and detoxing don't just happen overnight. There is no quick fix and any diet or detox program promising you one should be viewed with suspicion.

To support and assist your body's natural daily detox routine carried out by the liver you may consider a detox diet that lasts no longer than three days. Continuous deep detoxing for lengthy periods can be more harmful to your health in that your body loses valuable proteins, minerals, vitamins, and water during a detox program.

A good starting point for detoxifying your body is to restrict your diet to fruit and veggies for a day or two. Thereafter, you may introduce lean meat. Cut out all fizzy drinks, alcohol, desserts, chocolates, and sugar in your coffee or tea. Cut down and gradually restrict all starches.

When Not to Fast

There are times when fasting is not recommended for a person, no matter how used to fasting they may be. If your fasting day comes around and you are feeling any of the following symptoms, fasting that day will not be advisable for you. Knowing when to decide not to fast is important for your health and wellbeing.

If you are feeling sick, including nausea, diarrhea, and general feelings of sickness, take that day or the next few days off of fasting until you are feeling one hundred percent better. Your body needs all of the nutrition it can get while it is trying to fight off sickness and fasting will be taxing to the body, which will make it very difficult for it to fight off the illness.

If you are feeling weak to the point of not being able to do normal daily tasks, then fasting is not a good idea. Fasting can leave you feeling more tired and having less mental clarity. Doing so when you already feel extreme fatigue will only make this worse. Eating a regular and balanced food during the day will have many more benefits for your body than fasting in this case.

Foods to Eat and Avoid

Intermittent fasting only works if you eat the right kind of food. You need to make sure that you eat healthy food that gives you enough calories and makes you feel full. Here, we will discuss some of the food you should consider including in your diet alongside your fasting regimen so you can optimize your weight loss without compromising your health.

Good Food

- Veggies: kale, spinach, sweet potato, bell peppers, lettuce, Chinese cabbage, violet cabbage, scallions, turnip, beetroot, cauliflower, cabbage, broccoli, and carrot for veggies.

- Fruits: acai berries, gooseberries, blueberries, strawberries, tangerine, lime, lemon, plum, peach, tomato, cucumber, grapefruit, orange, banana, apple, and a limited number of mangoes should be eaten.
- Protein: eggs, tofu, beans and legumes, mushroom, fish, lean cuts of pork and beef, and chicken breast.
- Dairy: cottage cheese, homemade ricotta cheese, buttermilk, feta cheese, cheddar cheese, low-fat yogurt, and low-fat milk.
- Fats and oils: almond butter, peanut butter, sunflower butter, olive oil, rice bran oil, and edible grade coconut oil.
- Nuts and seeds: melon seeds, pumpkin seeds, sunflower seeds, macadamia, pistachios, pine nuts, pecan, almond, and walnut.
- Herbs and spices: clove, garlic powder, cardamom, star anise, allspice, chili flakes, white pepper, black pepper, cayenne pepper, turmeric, cumin, coriander, onion, ginger, garlic, oregano, thyme, rosemary, fennel, dill, mint, and cilantro.
- Drinks: plain water, homemade lemonade or electrolyte, coconut water, cold-pressed juices, and freshly pressed fruit juice.

As you can probably tell, you are already spoiled for choices here, even when you fast. With these, you can cook up some delectable dishes for yourself as a reward for your hard work. Of course, these are generally what you should eat.

Overall, I advise eating a healthy and balanced diet. Still, don't limit yourself to this list. We know what is good for our body and what isn't. However, certain details will differ for everyone.

For example, someone trying to gain muscle will have different nutritional needs than someone who is trying to lose weight. Therefore, I highly recommend deciding what your goals are and using calculators as well as your own research to discover what you need to eat in order to reach those goals.

The same goes for your dietary preferences. A vegan will have a very different diet in order to meet all their nutritional needs versus someone who eats animal products. Again, this requires more research depending on your goals, dietary preferences, current health, etc. There is no one-size-fits-all kind of diet.

Bad Food

- Fruits: any fruits rich in GI, such as grapes, jackfruit, pineapples, and mangoes.
- Protein: fatty cuts of pork and beef, and bacon (especially bacon).
- Dairy products: full-fat milk, full-fat yogurt, cream cheese, and flavored yogurt.
- Fats and oils: mayonnaise, margarine, butter, vegetable oil, lard, dalda, and hemp seed oil.
- Wholegrains: white rice, etc. Consume it in limited quantity and always eat it with at least five other veggies in the previous list to balance it out with the GI.
- Processed foods: salami, ranch dip, sausages, fries, jellies, bottled jams, etc.
- Drinks: fruit and vegetable juices, soda, diet soda (it doesn't help) and energy drinks.

This is not to say that you absolutely have to cut out all the food above. Of course, you can enjoy treats every now and then, but as a general rule, try and aim for 80% of the food you eat to be making you healthier and feel great. Certain types of fasting certainly give you leeway when it comes to food choices, but in terms of longevity and micronutrient intake, it is definitely best to develop a healthy and balanced diet.

Now that you know what to avoid, let us discuss how you could design your meal so that you do not lose your head while dieting.

What to Include in Your Meals?

Consider this a general guide as to what a meal should look like to you.

- Five types of veggies
- Three types of fruits
- Lean protein, but you can eat some red meat once in a while
- Lots of plant protein like kidney beans, seeds, nuts, garbanzo beans, and whole pulses (if you are a vegetarian)
- A few unsalted nuts, only a few
- A piece of 80% dark chocolate, if you need to

- Fruits, sour cream, or yogurt if you want some more sweet treats
- Alternatively, you can bake and store brownies that have healthy ingredients and less sugar
- Keep yourself hydrated—you limit your calorie intake, not your fluid intake; stay well hydrated as this is one of the only things that keep you going
- Alternatively, you can drink three or four cups of green tea during your fasting period

These are just some simple guidelines to help you plan your meals. You should strive to create a meal plan that is both healthy and delicious for you, meeting all your nutritional needs as well as your personal goals. The end result should be you leading a healthy and sustainable lifestyle. Depending on your medical history or dietary preference, I recommend you do additional research and consult your doctor. For instance, if you are a vegan, I recommend you check out a complete vegan nutrition guide if you haven't already. That way, you will know how to optimize your diet. The same advice for those who love to eat meat.

This may sound like a lot of work, however, understanding what you put in your body and why is essential to developing a long-term sustainable lifestyle, which is key to long-term weight loss and health and is, therefore, certainly worth the time and effort required. As many have said across the ages, our health is our greatest wealth.

CHAPTER 8:

Intermittent Fasting and Smoothies

Drinking smoothies on a daily basis is an easy way to eat a variety of fruits and vegetables which are full of fiber, vitamins, minerals and water. Eating our water from fruits and vegetables naturally hydrates our cells and tissues and helps restore youthful, glowing skin with another advantage of alkalizing your body and helping with weight loss and other diseases. Although some vegetables and fruits are more alkalizing than others, we can all benefit from their differences and nutritional qualities.

Blending pulverizes and breaks down the food so small which helps you absorb most of the nutrients from the fruits and vegetables. This is important because most of us have impaired digestion. This limits your body's ability to absorb all the nutrients from vegetables. Blending will help to "pre-digest" them for you, so you will receive most of the nutrition.

Unfortunately, some people think that drinking juices are not ideal due to the sugars present in the ingredients, fruits in particular. Then again, a lot of experts believe that drinking juices can actually be beneficial to people with diabetes.

In fact, certain vegetables and fruits are found to be helpful in improving the ability of the body to respond to insulin and control diabetes. Also, juicing can help these people lose weight, thus, allowing them to manage and Treat Type 2 diabetes.

If you have diabetes, you can drink juices to improve your health. However, you have to be cautious since natural sugars can still cause the glucose levels in your blood to rise. If you do not want to have these complications, you have to keep your blood glucose levels at bay.

Fructose, glucose, and sucrose are carbohydrates referred to as simple sugars. Fructose is natural sugar present in fruits. Glucose is sugar that is produced by your body when it breaks down the carbohydrates that you have consumed. Sucrose is a combination of fructose and glucose. When you consume sugar, your blood glucose levels rise.

Since fruits have fructose that can cause your blood glucose levels to rise, you should just opt for vegetables when juicing. Plenty of vegetables can give you all the vitamins and minerals you need without the carbohydrates. Fruits, as you know, can contain carbohydrates. If you are diabetic, you have to watch your intake of carbohydrates and sugar carefully.

Some people also argue that juicing takes away the fiber present in vegetables and fruits. Fiber is very important as it helps regulate blood sugar. If there is no fiber present in the juice you drink, your body will only receive the sugar content. Then again, experts say otherwise. According to them, juicing does not necessarily take all the fiber away from produce.

Vegetables contain fiber and not much carbohydrates, so you can have as many as you want without worrying about your diabetes.

In fact, certain vegetables are highly effective in managing diabetes. Cauliflower, Brussels sprouts, cucumber, and tomatoes, for instance, can help you manage your condition. Asparagus is also helpful in regulating levels of blood sugar. Carrots, collard greens, celery, parsley, cabbage, endive, beet greens, spinach, and broccoli are great sources of manganese.

Manganese can help you lower your insulin resistance, as well as improve your glucose metabolism. You can also get manganese from fruits, such as blueberries, strawberries, and pineapples. Broccoli is a highly recommended vegetable for people who want to prevent the onset of diabetes.

People who have diabetes are advised to have three to five servings of non-starchy vegetables on a daily basis. These vegetables have few carbohydrates and a low glycemic index. They can help promote stable and healthy levels of glucose in the blood. Take note that half a cup of vegetable juice is equal to one serving of raw, whole vegetables.

This makes juicing a great idea for dealing with diabetes. Consuming just a couple of servings of vegetables and drinking a glass of vegetable juice each day is enough to sustain your body with the nutrients it needs. You can use a cold press juicer to squeeze out the juice from fruits and vegetables. Cold pressing does not destroy the nutrients and enzymes present in the fruits and vegetables because it does not produce friction or heat.

Anyway, vegetables and fruits are not the only ones you can juice. Spices and herbs can also be juiced to help you deal with your diabetes. Cinnamon, for instance, is one of the most commonly used spices for treating diabetes. According to researchers at the University of Hanover, cinnamon can help lower blood glucose levels.

Other herbs that you can use to treat your diabetes include bitter melon, garlic, ginseng, fenugreek, and ginkgo. Cinnamon is also believed to be beneficial in lowering blood glucose levels by increasing insulin sensitivity.

Obesity is actually one of the factors that contribute to Type 2 diabetes. Unfortunately, a huge percentage of the American population is obese or overweight. This is why experts recommend certain juices and smoothies for weight loss. If you maintain your ideal weight, you will be able to avoid Type 2 diabetes.

In order to help Americans, understand sugar consumption further, the American Heart Association has provided guidelines regarding sugar intake. According to them, your added sugar should not be more than half of your unrestricted calories per day. Hence, you should carefully watch what you consume.

Women should not consume more than one hundred calories per day. This is equivalent to thirty grams or six teaspoons of sugar. Men, on the other hand, should not consume more than one hundred and fifty calories per day. This is equivalent to forty-five grams or nine teaspoons of sugar. Such sugars include high fructose corn syrups and other types of refined sugars.

Ingredients to Use in Making Smoothies

Green apple is an ideal ingredient. It can help slow down the digestion of carbohydrates and stimulate your pancreas. It can also help in slow glucose absorption. Green apples are better options than red apples for juicing because they have less sugar. However, you should still be cautious of your usage of green apples. Even though they are lower in sugar, you should still just use them sparingly.

Other ingredients you can use to regulate and stabilize your blood sugar levels are asparagus and green beans. Bitter melon is also great since it contains polypeptide p, oleanolic acid, glycosides, and charantin, which are efficient in lowering blood sugar. You can also use blueberries due to the phytochemicals they contain. They can help improve insulin sensitivity and even the onset of Type 2 diabetes.

When juicing for diabetes, see to it that you have lots of vitamin C. Broccoli is actually rich in vitamin C. In fact, it contains more vitamin C than oranges. It is also rich in beta-carotene and promotes good eyesight. In addition, it contains anti-inflammatory and detoxing properties. Carrots are rich in beta-carotene, as well. Plus, they can help improve and stimulate your liver. They can also help reduce your insulin resistance.

Nonetheless, carrots are quite high in sugar, which is why you should go easy on them. Celery is another great choice for juicing. It can help flush away uric acid from your digestive system. Cranberries are good too, since they can help fight against inflammation. They are advisable for people who are struggling with diabetes. Red grapefruit is also ideal due to its antioxidants that help in lowering high levels of blood sugar.

Red onions are excellent sources of antioxidants too. So, they are also effective in keeping your blood sugar at bay. What's more, you can use French green beans. Experts agree that these vegetables are effective in reducing pressure in the eyes and preventing macular degeneration. They are ideal to be juiced at least four times a day. You can easily grow your own French green beans in your backyard. Just provide a trellis for these beans to climb on.

If you want to protect your liver, raise your glutathione a bit, and enjoy the benefits of antioxidants, you can use milk thistle. Just like the ingredients already mentioned above, it is also ideal for juicing. If you like raspberries, you are in luck as they also make excellent choices for juicing. They can help you prevent macular degeneration. They can also help reduce inflammation since they are rich in antioxidants.

Do not forget to consider spinach, tomatoes, and watermelon when juicing for diabetes. Spinach contains antioxidants and anti-inflammatory agents, such as beta-carotene. Tomatoes can help regulate your levels of blood sugar. They are rich in lycopene, a beneficial antioxidant for diabetics. Watermelon can efficiently lower your blood pressure. Diabetics, as you know, have to watch their blood pressure regularly.

Furthermore, you should include cabbages, avocados, and udos oil in your juices. Squash are rich in vitamins A, B, C, as well as iron and calcium. Hence, it can help you treat diabetes, improve your eyesight, and help with your cardiovascular issues. Asparagus is ideal too. It is rich in fiber and vitamins A and C. It can help control your blood sugar and lower your cholesterol levels.

Fresh vegetables have a lot of biophotons, which make them excellent in treating diabetes. If you want to use other fruits and vegetables, that is totally fine. Just see to it that you use a greater proportion of vegetables over sweet fruits, such as pineapples and apples. Find out the sugar content of the fruits or vegetables you want to use.

Pears are recommended to people with diabetes because these fruits contain levulose. It is a natural sugar that is more easily tolerated by the bodies of those who have diabetes. You have to follow your ideal sugar consumption, so you can live a long, happy life.

Fruits and vegetables are indeed excellent sources of the vitamins and minerals that diabetics need to improve their condition. Nonetheless, you can also add other ingredients to your juice. This will allow you to experiment with your juices and smoothies, so you will not be bored with the same beverage you have on a regular basis. Once again, see to it that you use these ingredients in moderation.

Also, if you have any allergies to these ingredients, be sure to contact your doctor. Surely, you do not want to have skin breakouts or experience unpleasant side effects. You should also ask the opinion of your doctor with regard to your plan of juicing for diabetes. Have yourself checked up, so you can find out if you are really fit for juicing. Your doctor may even be able to suggest ingredients for your juices and smoothies.

Red sea salt, for instance, contains seventy-six minerals from the sea, including sodium chloride. This makes it a whole lot better than regular table salt. You can also use concentrated sea minerals. Using one-half teaspoon of these sea minerals in your juice can significantly improve its taste.

You can also use chlorella to help regulate your blood sugar and help prevent high blood pressure or hypertension. Coconut oil is another recommended ingredient for juices and smoothies for diabetes. It contains fatty acids that can provide energy for your brain. As you know, high levels of insulin can prevent your brain from getting sufficient sugar. Good thing, your brain can also use fat as a source of fuel.

Coconut oil contains fats that can fuel your brain and even prevent Alzheimer's disease. Remember to keep your jar of coconut oil on your stove or somewhere with a temperature of at least seventy-six degrees so it stays liquid. Of course, you should also consume your juice or smoothie immediately once you added the coconut oil into it. Otherwise, the coconut oil will start to turn into solid.

Herbs that Help the Body to Purify Itself

Herbs, together with a conscientious lifestyle, have power. Many herbs are powerful detoxifiers. Many rare herbs are available only locally, e.g. in Africa or Siberia but are unavailable or even unheard of in other parts of the world. This explains why there are so many different "best detox herbs" lists.

If you want a healthy and active life, it's essential to learn about plants and herbs that may help you.

- **Agave**

This description has little effect on where these plants tend to grow, but due to their ability to thrive in dry areas with little water, they can be found in many desert regions worldwide. They do not have a lot of resistance to cultivation and can be grown anywhere as long as there is sufficient water available throughout the year. The following fact is about solvents and uses.

Agaves are mostly evergreen succulent plants in which all the leaves are reduced to a single plate called the "crown" at the top of the plant. The branches are short and stout and produce a single or pair of leaves called 'culms.' Agaves have greenish-gray or black stems with small (often white) spines in clusters at regular intervals along with them.

- **Alder**

Alder is a common name, full name Alnus, description deciduous or semi-deciduous trees found worldwide in the northern hemisphere. This hardy tree's wood is used as fuel and for making furniture, charcoal, and oars. The medicinal parts are alder bark and leaves. Areas of resistance to cultivation are poorly drained soil, particularly wet peaty areas, common throughout Europe but not native to North America.

Alder bark gives its positivity(power) as an anti-inflammatory by inhibiting prostaglandins' production (steroids that stimulate inflammation). It also contains other anti-inflammatory compounds such as flavonoids (in sub-form: also) and tannins. An oil (including over 20% fatty acid esters of caffeic acid) is obtained from the expressed alder leaves and called "Alnus maritima" oil.

Alder berries are used to make jellies, jams, and liquors. They have a silky texture and are eaten raw or ripe or made into pies. They can be crushed and used for digestion problems; the oil from them has mild sedative qualities. The alder's bark is used to make toothpaste, and the inner bark contains tannins used in tanning leather.

Alder tree: "Alnus glutinosa" and "Alnus incana." Parts used: Alder bark. Method of preparation: Collected in August/September, dried by air, extracted using water or ethanol 95% +water 5% (1:9). What is the method of preparing this medicine? 1–2 drops daily before food, maximum three times a day. Solutions can be stored in dark bottles at five °C for up to three years without losing activity.

- **Alfalfa**

It has been eaten as green for at least 3,000 years. Native Area: Widespread throughout southern Europe and much of Asia and Africa; cultivated and naturalized in many other regions. A hardy herbaceous perennial of the pea family Fabaceae. It is extensively grown as silage, fodder, hay, and green manure for many livestock species. Native Area: Widespread throughout the temperate regions of the world; naturalized in the various areas. An annual or perennial herb of the pea family Fabaceae, native to Europe and Western Asia. A small shrub or herb of the mint family Labiatae with aromatic leaves, used as vegetables and herbs.

- **Aloe**

This herb is often used to treat burns, scrapes, or other skin conditions such as acne. It contains toxins that can work gently within the body and promote ultimate healing. Much research has been done on aloe vera's effectiveness in promoting healthy skin and weight loss thanks to its ability to increase metabolism and burn fat while helping with cell regeneration.

This succulent plant has numerous health benefits, including treatment for burns, diabetes, psoriasis, etc. It was used in ancient times as a standard remedy for many different ailments, and it still holds today. A word of caution, though – there are toxins in this plant that can be harmful to humans. Avoid using fresh juice of aloe vera. This herb should never be ingested without the supervision of a health care provider.

Aloe is the common name for over 400 different succulent plant species, often called "aloes" in several regions.

The aloe is a genus of flowering plants belonging to the asphodel family Asphodelaceae. There are over 400 known species of aloe. This genus includes both desert and tropical forest species, and only 14 out of the 400 have found medicinal properties so far. Aloes tend to grow in dry climates with sandy soil that has no humus content whatsoever. The majority of them are found in Africa and South Asia, but some aloes can be grown as houseplants anywhere it's warm year-round, or there's an artificial heating system.

The name "Aloe" is of Greek origin: a, meaning "without," and loess, meaning "a lot." It refers to the typical absence of leaves within the genus. Aloe uses simple, tubular, unbranched stems to get around. Aloe flowers are tubular with multiple anthers opening onto a central funnel-like stigma. Some aloes have sharp or saw-toothed leaves, while others are smooth.

Aloe is the common name of many succulent plants. This genus is classified under "Asphodelaceae," a family comprising semievergreen, perennial, and short-lived plants with ephemeral flowers. Aloes are distributed worldwide from tropics to temperate regions and are commonly cultivated in tropical and subtropical gardens. They have many uses, such as food items, medicine, and cosmetics.

- **Amaranth**

Amaranth is a flowering plant in the family Amaranthaceae. The name is also used collectively for all members of this family. The scientific name, Amaranthus, means "never-fading" or "unwilling," with a probable reference to the flower's everlasting flowers and ability to survive harsh seasons as an annual plant.

The description of amaranth depends on whether it is being used with its common name or its scientific name. Amaranth has many variations under its common name, but they are all dark green, sometimes reddish color leafy vegetables that can be eaten cooked or raw when young and tender. It's a popular vegetable among vegetarians and vegans because of its high nutritional value, never spoiling quality, and ease of cultivation.

As a cereal grain, there are two main types of Amaranth. The first type is called the "grain amaranth." It can be used in much the same way as rice and is commonly grown in China for that reason. The second type is called "pseudo-cereal" amaranth, which is more widely known as "quinoa," named after a South American tribe that used it to make bread. Both grain amaranth and pseudo-cereal amaranth can be cooked similar to cooking rice or quinoa.

- **Amla**

Amla is one of the most common Ayurvedic herbs used to treat diabetes and a common remedy for improving circulation, health, and skin. It is also used in hair coloring. The dried fruits can be mixed with milk and consumed to improve kidney function.

- **Angelica**

This herb contains substances that help decrease anxiety and stress. It can also help with insomnia, partly due to its ability to relax the body and promote restful sleep during the night.

There are four types of angelicas, similar in appearance but different in range and uses. American angelica (A. atropurpurea) is one of the best-known medicinal herbs used for coughs and colds. Umbelliferous angelicas include A. dahurica, A. sylvestris, and A. crenata; these were more popular with earlier herbalists than today because they contain much less medicinally active volatile oils than does American angelica or European angelica (A. archangelica). In general, angelica is a hardy, drought- and frost-resistant perennial. It has smooth, erect stems with alternate leaves that are finely dissected into many narrow segments. The leaves taste bitter when fresh and turn dark as they dry; the leaf volatile oil's fragrance resembles carrot seed oil. The flowers are borne in umbels atop the stems; they are white at first but later take on a pinkish tint. American angelica (A. atropurpurea) is sometimes cultivated on a large scale to extract its volatile oils. Angelica can be found in many parts of the world, especially in hilly areas. In western Europe, this herb is grown mainly in the Alps and Pyrenees. The plant grows in China, the Caucasus, Russia, Turkey, and central Europe. Angelica leaf and root, which are used for tonic and potherb.

Characteristics of Tonic and Potherb:

a) Tonic, stomachic, cold.
b) Potherb, stomachic, hot.

Angelica is also traditionally used in the home remedy of alleviating the symptoms of enuresis (incontinence), kidney stones (obstructions) in the urinary tract. The plant's root has been used as a purgative to treat menstrual disorders due to its high potassium salts frequency.

- **Arsesmart**

A bushy herb with large leaves that are oviform or oblong-lanceolate. The leaves are dark green and covered in minute scabrous dots. The leaves grow up to about 8 inches in length and 3 inches in width. At the end of each plate, arises a small sharp thorn approximately 1/4 the size of the leaf. It is an annual herb as well as a dicot.

- **Asafoetida**

It should also be used with some caution during a fever when the stomach is upset or has a history of irritable bowel syndrome.

- **Bach Flower**

They contain substances that can help promote positive thinking as well as the reduction of inflammation and pain. Certain species of this herb are considered natural tranquilizers, while others contain adaptogens that help restore normal physiological functioning.

- **Bacopa**

Sometimes called "Indian ginseng," bacopa is an herb known to promote healthy brain functions. It contains substances that help promote healthy neurons and blood flow while also helping with mood balance.

- **Basil**

An herb often found in Italian cuisine. This herb can be used as a plate garnish as well as eaten raw atop salads or sandwiches.

It contains a eugenol substance that gives it an antifungal property and more antioxidant power than vitamin E. This herb is often used in many recipes for cooking and herbal remedies for the skin.

- **Bay Leaf**

This herb has been used as a scent, flavoring, or medicinal agent for thousands of years, mainly due to its antibiotic properties and ability to relieve pain.

It is generally used in cooking and as an ingredient in herbal remedies to treat stomach aches, diarrhea, or upset stomach.

- **Beggar's Buttons**

Description: It is a biennial herb with a rosette of leaves in the first year and a tall flowering stem in the second. The roots have been used as a blood purifier. Native Area: Northern Europe/ Siberia; throughout North America and northern Eurasia. Traditionally they are widely used for gastrointestinal inflammation and disorders, including colitis and other inflammatory bowel conditions.Medicinal parts: Roots. Medicinal uses Diuretic, nervous system stimulant, blood purifier.

- **Bilberry**

The leaves, fruits, and flowers of this herb are rich in vitamins A and C and the anthocyanins that give it a deep blue color. These nutrients have been known to increase eye health as well as treat urinary tract infections. They also support heart health due to their antioxidants properties which will help prevent stroke and cardiovascular disease.

- **Birch**

This herb's leaves are often used to provide relief from a sore throat, dry skin, urinary tract problems, and digestive issues. The birch tree's bark is used as an ingredient in cough syrups and teas for the same reasons. All parts of this herb are high in salicin, which reduces inflammation of arthritic joints and pain and discomfort caused by rheumatism or arthritis.

- **Blackberry**

The berries are used as medicine. It can also be found in cultivated gardens. Native Area: Eastern United States. The part of the plant used/Medicinal part: Berries. Medicinal uses Antirheumatic, diuretic (kidney), purgative.

- **Black Cohosh**

The root is used as medicine. It can also be found in cultivated gardens. Medicinal uses: Antirheumatic, antispasmodic, antiseptic (externally), cholagogue, diaphoretic, emmenagogue, nervine(nerve), stimulant(sedative), tonic (uterus).

- **Black Locust**

A perennial tree native to North America is found in open woods and roadsides. The bark is used as medicine. It can also be found in cultivated gardens. Native Area: Eastern North America; more common in the southern states. The part of the plant used/Medicinal part: Bark

- **Blackwork**

A perennial herb native to Europe, it is found in woods and meadows. Native Area: Western Europe; throughout North America and northern Eurasia. Medicinal part: Leaves, seeds, flowers (dried). Medicinal uses Antirheumatic (prevents stiffness and inflammation), anti-inflammatory, astringent, diuretic (kidney, urinary tract), expectorant, stimulant (circulatory effects).

- **Black Willow**

A small tree native to North America is found in swamps and edges of marshes. The bark is used as medicine. It can also be found in cultivated gardens.

Native Areas: Eastern North America; more common in the southern states. The part of the plant used/Medicinal part: Bark

Medicinal uses Antirheumatic, astringent (vulnerary), diuretic (kidney), sedative, tonic (nervous).

Medicinal parts: Bark. Medicinal uses Febrifuge, sedative, tonic.

- **Blue-Eyed Grass**

It is an herbaceous plant with pinnately divided leaves; it has been used as a purgative and styptic agent—native Area: Eastern North America; more common in the southern states.

Blue Vervain

It helps with pain control and has been used for centuries in teas for several ailments, including migraines or headaches, insomnia or sleep disorders, rheumatism, and arthritis inflammation. It can also be boiled with other herbs for helping with digestion, such as gas or nausea.

- **Boneset**

Boneset is a flowering plant that has been known to help treat fevers, colds, and flu but should not be used while pregnant due to its toxicity. It can also help reduce inflammation, such as that from an appendix or kidney stones' irritation. The leaves can also be used to help with respiratory infections.

- **Borage**

This herb's rhizomes are used as a skin lotion to treat inflammation, while the flowers and leaves can support healthy blood pressure levels and lower cholesterol. It is also an excellent alternative for those who suffer from digestive issues such as diarrhea, constipation, or bloating due to its diuretic properties. This herb should not be used with pharmaceutical drugs or antacids meant to treat heart conditions as it may reduce the effectiveness of these medications.

- **Burdock**

A perennial herb native to North America is found in open fields and roadsides. The root is used as medicine. It can also be found in cultivated gardens. Native Area: Eastern United States. The part of the plant used/Medicinal part: Root Medicinal uses: Cleansing, decongestant, diuretic, emetic (potent), expectorant, a stimulant.

Medicinal parts: Flowers/leaves. Medicinal Uses Antispasmodic, carminative, diuretic (kidney and liver), emollient, febrifuge, hypotensive, nervine, sedative, tonic.

Burdock root is an herb used for years by Traditional Chinese Medicine (TCM) practitioners for its cleansing and detoxifying properties helping to clear heat/metabolism stagnation from the principal organs of elimination.

- **Calendula**

It can also help with skin conditions such as acne, eczema, psoriasis, and dermatitis. It can also be boiled with other herbs for treating wounds or rashes.

- **Casticote**

Casticote comes from a plant in the parsley family known as Lespedeza that grows wild in eastern Asia. This herb can be used to treat sore throats and make tea from the plant for treating diarrhea.

- **Catnip**

Helps relieve pain in various situations, including headaches, joint aches or pains, and menstrual cramps and headaches.

- **Celery Seed**

Celery seeds are very high in a substance that can inhibit blood clotting. Pregnant or breastfeeding women should avoid this herb due to its high amount of phytosterols that may interfere with hormone production.

- **Centaury**

Centaury is another ancient herb used for treating ailments such as phlebitis, asthma, and rheumatism

- **Chamomile**

Many varieties of the chamomile plant include German, Roman, English, and Hungarian. This herb's flowers are often used to make a soothing tea used to treat a fever, allergies, and relaxation. This herb should not be consumed while pregnant or breastfeeding due to its high amount of phytosterols which interferes with hormones in the body.

Chamomile Flower Oil is a natural product that is very easy to prepare. There are three types of chamomile extract oil: steam distilled, cold-pressed and chemical. The moisture purified extracts contain most of the chamomile flower oil components, followed by cold-pressed chamomile extract. Chemical extracted oils don't hold as much of the active compounds found in the steam distilled or cold-pressed extracts.

It can also be boiled with other herbs for treating headaches.

- **Chasteberry**

The chaste berry is a small fruit that comes from a bush native to Europe. This herb is often used to treat sore throats as well as to ease nausea. It can also be used for bladder infections and urinary tract problems.

- **Chicory**

This herb's roots are used for treating stomach ulcers and can also help with swollen lymph glands. The chicory plant leaves are often blended with other herbs such as sage and thyme to make an herbal tea used to treat bronchitis and pneumonia. This herb should not be consumed by those who have a history of heart conditions or high blood pressure as it may interfere with these conditions.

- **Chili**

This plant's fleshy fruit is derived from the pepper family and belongs to the same family as chili peppers. Chilies are used to make a tea used to treat digestive problems such as fever and indigestion. No one with a functional heart condition should consume chili as it can lower the level of potassium in the body, which may be detrimental to the heart.

- **Chrysanthemum**

It is commonly used in teas to help with sleep, backache, and coughs. It can also be applied topically for cuts, scrapes, or other types of skin conditions such as burns.

- **Cinnamon**

This is a spice derived from a plant that is native to Sri Lanka. Cinnamon is often used in cooking, and some cultures flavor their foods with it. It works by getting rid of excess phlegm by decreasing the amount of fluid in the lungs and throat. Doing this helps an individual breathe easier and cough less often, while also reducing a cold or fever chills.

The bark has been used as a spice for flavoring various foods and beverages for many years—native Areas: Southern Asia, Papua New Guinea, and Indonesia.

The dried fruit of the plant has been used medicinally for various purposes. Native Area: Pakistan. The part of the plant used/Medicinal part: Fruit. Medicinal uses Antimicrobial (bactericidal, fungicidal, etc.), carminative (gas), laxative (antispasmodic), stimulant (circulatory effects).

- **Citronella**

This herb comes from a type of lemongrass which grows in East Africa, Southeast Asia, China, and India. It is used as an insect repellent or a deodorizer.

INTERMITTENT FASTING AND AUTOPHAGY

- **Clove**

This spice comes from a flower that is grown in Indonesia, China, and Malaysia. It is used as a flavor in cooking and also to burn as a mosquito repellent.

This plant grows in the United States and Canada and has many uses, including helping cure coughs.

- **Columbine**

Full Name: Aquilegia vulgaris L. Description: A perennial herb native to the Eastern United States is found in open woods and thickets. The dried flowers have been used as an eye remedy. It can also be found in cultivated gardens.

Native Area: Eastern North America; more common in the southern states. The part of the plant used/Medicinal part: Flowers. Medicinal uses Antirheumatic, diuretic (kidney), expectorant, nervine (nervous system).

- **Comfrey**

Helps with pain control as well as inflammatory issues such as rheumatism, arthritis, or gout. It can also be boiled with other herbs to help with stomach aches or gas.

- **Dandelion**

It can also be boiled with other herbs to improve bowel movements, reduce flatulence, and promote a healthy uterus for women who may be pregnant or trying to conceive.

- **Dill**

This herb is often used to help with pain or inflammation in various situations, including joint aches and pains, migraines or headaches, and more. It can be boiled with other herbs to help with indigestion or abdominal cramping and promote healthy bowel movements.

It should be noted that dill is not meant to be eaten raw.

- ## Echinacea

This herb is known as "purple coneflower" and comes in the form of teas, tinctures, extracts, or capsules that help promote healthy immune system responses. It can also be applied topically for cuts, scrapes, or other types of skin conditions such as acne.

- ## Elderberry

A deciduous shrub native to Europe, it is found in woods and meadows. The white flowers are followed by blue-black berries which are used as medicine. It can also be found in cultivated gardens. Native Area: Europe and Western Asia; cultivated worldwide, especially for its ornamental value and fruit. Medicinal parts: Berries, flowers, leaves. Medicinal uses: Antirheumatic, antiseptic (topical), astringent, anxiolytic (calms the mind), diaphoretic, febrifuge, hypotensive (lowers blood pressure), nervine(nerve), purgative, sedative, vulnerary.

- ## Elder

A deciduous shrub is native to North America. It is found in woods and along streams. It can also be found in cultivated gardens. Native Area: Eastern North America; more common in the southern states. Medicinal parts: Berries, flowers, leaves. Medicinal uses Antirheumatic, antiseptic (topical), astringent, anxiolytic (calms the mind), diaphoretic, febrifuge, hypotensive (lowers blood pressure), nervine(nerve), sedative.

- ## Ephedra

This herb is known as "ma huang" or "ma huang seed," and it is commonly used to promote healthy energy levels. It can also be boiled with other herbs to relieve pain or inflammation in various situations such as joint aches, headaches, tension headaches, or more.

- ## Eyebright

This herb contains substances that help reduce glaucoma symptoms caused by elevated pressure within the eyeball.

- **Fennel**

Most well-known is to be used as a flavoring in Italian dishes. It also helps increase milk production when women are breastfeeding, makes tea for secretion, and is an herbal remedy for bronchitis or asthma.

- **Feverfew**

It was helping to reduce the symptoms of migraines, headaches, or tension headaches. It can also be applied topically for cuts, scrapes, or other types of skin conditions such as burns. It can also be boiled with other herbs to help with indigestion, abdominal cramping, or nausea.

- **Feverwort**

This herb comes in a tea form with many uses, including joint pain, headaches, stress, and anxiety. It can be applied topically for eczema.

- **Garlic**

This spice comes from the bulb part of garlic plants grown in large amounts across various large areas of the globe. It is commonly used in cooking because it has been shown to have many health benefits and medicinal properties that help control blood pressure when taken for long periods.

- **Gingko**

This tree grows in the United States and is also grown in other parts of the world.

- **Ginseng**

This herb comes in a tea form, tincture, or extract that helps promote healthy energy levels while helping to relax muscles and increase blood flow to the brain. It can also be applied topically for cuts, scrapes, or other types of skin conditions such as burns.

- **Goldenrod, Ragweed**

Goldenrod has its place in nature. It also works by surrounding the brain with its active chemicals, which help reduce stress levels.

This herb is often used for preventing rheumatism because it contains compounds that help restore normal physiological functioning. It has been boiled with other herbs for treating joint pain, headaches, or migraines.

- **Goldenseal**

It is used today as an alternative to antibiotic agents due to its ability to fight infections. It is also used to make a tincture which can be applied topically for various skin conditions such as rashes and abscesses. It can also be boiled with other herbs to make a tea that helps treat coughs and colds.

- **Gotu Kola**

This herb is widely used in Ayurvedic medicine due to its antioxidant properties. It is also used to increase memory and concentration.

- **Grape Seed**

This seed is extracted from the fruit of a grape plant that has several uses and flavorful addition to recipes.

- **Ground Apple**

The dried leaves have been used as a gentle purgative and an alternative. The flowers can be made into tea. The root has astringent properties—native Area: Eastern North America; more common in the southern states.

- **Hawthorn Berries**

Hawthorn berries are often used in herbal remedies due to their high amount of flavonoids that can increase circulation, improve heart function and lower cholesterol. It is also used to ease pressure and pain in blocked arteries while lowering LDL cholesterol levels.

- **Hops**

This herb is often used in teas to help with insomnia as well as anxiety and stress. It can also be boiled with other herbs to help with indigestion, abdominal cramping, or nausea.

- **Horsetail**

This herb is often used in teas as well as herbal remedies to treat bronchitis and asthma. It also has been known to reduce inflammation of the ear and nose.

- **Hydrangea**

The leaves of this herb are used in tea for treating several things, including colds, tuberculosis, fever, arthritis, digestive issues, and infections.

- **Hyssop**

This herb is commonly known as a "Jewish Tea" due to its use in religious ceremonies. It can be used as herbal medicine to cure boils, bruises, and wounds. It should not be used by those with bleeding disorders or by those who are pregnant or breastfeeding due to its high amount of compounds that may interfere with hormone production in the body.

- **Inula**

It is used in treating issues such as chronic bronchitis, coughing, and allergies. It can also help lower blood pressure levels through the use of its properties known as flavonoids.

- **Ipecac**

It is often used to induce vomiting, which can help with removing harmful substances from the body.

- **Jasmine**

It is used to help with conditions such as asthma, stomach problems, and coughs. It can be applied topically to relieve swelling and reduce odor from some skin disorders such as eczema. It should not be applied topically to women who are pregnant or breastfeeding.

- **Kalanchoe**

The leaves of this herb are used for respiratory infections such as bronchitis and inflammation. It also has properties that can help with arthritis and pain.

- **Kava Coptic**

This herb comes in a tea form, capsule, or extract that helps promote relaxation by reducing mental and physical tension while easing anxiety and stress. It can also be applied topically for cuts, scrapes, or other types of skin conditions such as burns.

- **Lady's Thumb**

This herb is often used to help with pain control and for treatment for arthritis or gout. It can also be boiled with other herbs for stomach aches or gas.

This herb comes from a small plant native to Europe and Asia. A decoction is a general term used to describe a tea made by extracting the phytoactive compounds from plants, such as making a tincture.

- **Lavender**

This herb comes from a fragrant flower that is native to the Mediterranean. Still, it also has many other benefits: being helpful with confidence issues, anxiety, skin conditions such as dermatitis, and relaxation.

- **Lemon Balm**

This herb comes in a tea form with many uses, including pain control, stress, and anxiety. It can be boiled with other herbs to help with indigestion or abdominal cramping, or nausea.

This herb comes from a plant native to Africa, Europe, and Asia. It has many health benefits and can help with anxiety, stress, pain, skin conditions, etc.

- **Lemongrass**

This herb can treat some different ailments, including herpes, cold sores, and more.

- **Lemon Verbena**

It is used to help relieve pain in various situations and headaches, tension headaches, backaches, menstrual cramps, and more. It can also be boiled with other herbs for treating stomach aches or gas.

- **Licorice**

This herb is derived from the root of the plant Glycyrrhiza glabra, and it has many health benefits. It is often used for digestive issues such as diarrhea and gas and making a remedy that can help relieve nasal congestion due to allergies, congestion, or sinus infections when used topically.

The root is used to make medicine. Native Area: Eastern North America; more common in the southern states. The part of the plant used/Medicinal part: Roots. Medicinal uses Analgesic (pain reliever), anti-inflammatory, anti-tussive (cough suppressor), astringent, carminative (gas), diuretic (kidney), expectorant, laxative, stimulant (circulatory effects).

- **Linden**

It helps with stress and anxiety because of its many positive effects on the body, such as promoting blood circulation, easing tension in the muscles, and promoting restful sleep during the night. It can also be boiled with other herbs for helping with digestion, such as gas or nausea.

- **Lovage**

This herb comes in a tea form with many uses, including pain control, stress, and anxiety. It can also be boiled with other herbs to help with indigestion or abdominal cramping, or nausea.

- **Mahonia**

This herb comes from parts of the dogbane plant, which grow across the globe. It contains substances that are said to lower cholesterol levels and reduce the risk of certain types of cancer.

- **Manuka Honey**

This honey comes from the Manuka tree in New Zealand, and it has several uses, including helping to reduce inflammation in the body such as arthritis, gout, or rheumatism. It can also be boiled with other herbs for promoting healthy digestion.

- **Marjoram**

This herb is commonly used for various illnesses, such as relieving stomach issues like flatulence, constipation, diarrhea, or cramps. It has pain-relieving properties and can be applied topically to treat open wounds and skin conditions such as dermatitis.

- **Marshmallow**

A perennial herb native to Europe is found in roadsides, fields, and streams. The dried flowers have been used as medicine. Native Area: Western Europe; throughout North America and northern Eurasia. The part of the plant used/Medicinal part: Flowers. Medicinal uses Analgesic (pain reliever), diuretic (kidney), sedative, tonic - increases circulation to the brain and other vital organs.

- **Milk Thistle**

This herb comes from an annual wildflower native to the Mediterranean region. It has many uses, such as helping with liver problems by providing nutrients for the liver cells while also helping to activate liver enzymes to help break down drugs or toxins in the body that may be harmful.

The leaves, roots, and seeds from this herb contain substances that promote healthy liver functions while promoting healthy liver cell production. It has numerous uses, including helping to relieve pain in the body and many other health benefits, such as promoting a healthy mind and body. It can be used for cuts, scrapes, or different types of skin conditions such as burns.

- **Mint**

Mint also has a unique taste and taste that can be used in many dishes and eaten raw.

- **Mistletoe**

This herb is often used for respiratory conditions such as flues or colds. It can also be boiled with other herbs for treating stomach cramps, diarrhea, and more.

- **Monarda**

It reduces nausea or vomiting when you're sick because of its ability to increase saliva while also minimizing dehydration of the mouth and throat. It can also be boiled with other herbs to help with indigestion, abdominal cramping, or nausea.

- **Motherwort**

It can be used for burns or eaten in place of birth control due to its ability to slow down the heart rate so the body can rest when it needs time to heal.

- **Mullein**

This herb is also known as "hag's taper" because it was traditionally used to light Europe's lamps. It has also been used for treating earaches, ear infections, and other types of ear pain.

- **Myrrh**

This herb is sometimes used as an astringent or tincture for treating wounds. It can also be applied topically for cuts, scrapes, or other types of skin conditions such as burns.

- **Nettle**

This herb is often used for many things, including helping with cold or flu symptoms, arthritis, and urinary tract issues. It can be consumed or applied topically depending on the condition being treated.

This herb contains substances that can help promote good overall health and healing in the body. It can also be boiled with other herbs for promoting healthy digestion.

- **Oatstraw**

This herb is known as "oat grass," and it can help promote healthy digestion. It can also be boiled with other herbs to help with indigestion, abdominal cramping, or nausea.

- **Onion**

It helps relieve pain in various situations such as joint aches, headaches, tension headaches, or more. It can also be boiled with other herbs for promoting digestion, such as gas or nausea.

- **Oregano**

Oregano adds a unique flavor and spice to the dishes it's cooked in. It can also be eaten raw, but its flavor is much more potent when cooked before eating.

- **Ostrich Feathers**

These are used to make a soothing poultice for cuts, rashes, and burns while also having strong disinfectant properties and treating many types of infections. It can also be boiled with other herbs to help with indigestion, abdominal cramping, or nausea.

- **Parsley**

This herb is typically seen as a cooking ingredient, but it is also used to help with kidney disease, rheumatism, stomach pain, gout, and weight loss.

- **Passion Flower**

This herb has many uses but is most famous for its use in treating insomnia and anxiety. It can be consumed or applied topically depending on the condition being treated.

- **Peony**

Considered to be one of the most effective herbs that can heal urinary tract infections thanks to its ability to inhibit bacteria. It is also used to help treat red blood cell disorders such as anemia while increasing the body's oxygen levels.

- **Pennyroyal**

This herb is often used to encourage sweating which will help with the detoxification of the body. It also contains substances that can help lower cholesterol levels, ease menstrual cramps and reduce inflammation.

- **Peppermint**

This herb is often used for many conditions, including helping with stomachaches, indigestion, menstrual cramps, nausea, and more. It can also be applied topically for cuts, scrapes, or other skin conditions such as dermatitis and psoriasis.

It is also used to help relieve pain in various situations such as joint aches, headaches, tension headaches, or more. It can also be boiled with other herbs for promoting digestion, such as gas or nausea.

- **Pine**

It is often boiled with other herbs to make a decoction or tincture, which can be consumed or applied topically.

- **Plantain**

It is used as a tea that helps relieve pain and inflammation in the body by reducing swelling and inflammation in the joints and muscles and reducing fever. It can also be boiled with other herbs for promoting digestion, such as gas or nausea.

- **Poppy**

It is used as a tincture that helps promote healthy energy levels while promoting restful sleep during the night. It can also be boiled with other herbs for helping with digestion, such as gas or nausea.

These flowers are often used to help with pain such as menstrual cramps, toothaches, rheumatism, and sore muscles. They can also be applied topically for cuts, scrapes, or other types of injuries.

- **Prickly Ash**

It promotes healthy blood flow to all body organs, reducing pain and inflammation in muscles and joints, promoting healthy digestion, relieving menstrual cramps, relieving stomach aches, and more. It can also be applied topically for cuts, scrapes, or other types of skin conditions such as burns.

- **Prickly Pear**

This herb is derived from the fruit of a cactus native to South America and throughout the world today, where it grows in desert areas. It can be used for several disorders, including allergies and colic in babies and digestive issues. It can also be boiled with other herbs to provide relief from asthma and hay fever.

- **Purslane**

This herb is often used to help treat acne, psoriasis, dermatitis, eczema, and more. It has a calming effect on the nervous system, helping those who suffer from stress or anxiety, or even depression.

- **Red Clover**

This herb is commonly used in teas and drinks for many things, including digestive issues such as indigestion, flatulence, and diarrhea. It is also used in helping with pain control, stress, and anxiety. It can also be boiled with other herbs for treating indigestion, abdominal cramping, or nausea.

- **Rose**

It can also be applied topically for scars or burns while it has also been known to stimulate the immune system and provide antioxidants that can help slow down the aging process in the body.

- **Rosemary**

This herb is often used to suppress coughs, eliminate gas accumulation, improve digestion, and be used for headaches. It can also be used as an antibacterial for wounds, cuts, scrapes, or other types of skin conditions. Rosemary is typically used in Italian recipes but can also be eaten raw as a plate garnish with meals like meatballs.

- **Rue**

This herb comes in a tea form that helps relieve pain in various situations such as joint aches, headaches, tension headaches, or more. It can also be boiled with other herbs for treating indigestion, abdominal cramping, or nausea.

- **Rye**

This herb is used for several illnesses, including headaches and stomach cramps. It has also been known to reduce inflammation, particularly in the case of sprains or bruises.

- **Saffron**

This herb comes from a pretty flower known as "red gold," originating from southern Europe and Asia. It is often used to help with issues such as depression, anxiety, insomnia, and more. It can be consumed or applied topically depending on the condition being treated.

- **Sage**

This herb is commonly used to help with many things, including sore throats, coughs, and respiratory ailments. It can also be boiled with other herbs for treating digestive issues such as gas, nausea, diarrhea, and cramps.

It can also be boiled with other herbs to help with indigestion, abdominal cramping, or nausea.

- **Saint John's Wort**

It is used to help treat depression as well as muscle and joint aches or pain. It can also be boiled with other herbs to help with menstrual cramps.

This herb comes in a tea form that helps relieve pain and anxiety while also promoting restful sleep during the night. It can also be boiled with other herbs to help with indigestion, abdominal cramping, or nausea.

- **Sandalwood**

It is used to make a soothing poultice for cuts, rashes, and burns while also having strong disinfectant properties and treating many infections. It can also be boiled with other herbs for promoting healthy digestion, such as gas or nausea.

- **Sarsaparilla**

This herb has many uses, such as helping relieve pain due to arthritis or sprains or bruises and helping with stomach aches and diarrhea. It can also be boiled with other herbs to make a decoction or tincture.

- **Schizandra**

It can also be boiled with other herbs to promote healthy liver functions, such as replacing damaged tissue and upgrading a healthy mind and body.

- **Scullcap**

It is often used in teas for various things, including anxiety, depression, insomnia, and migraines. It can also be applied topically to relieve pain such as arthritic pain.

- **Shepherd's Purse**

It is used in teas to help with fevers and other infections in the body. It can also be boiled with other herbs to help with indigestion, abdominal cramping, or nausea.

- **Silverweed**

A perennial herb native to Western Europe, it is found in woods and thickets. The flowers are pink, and the leaves are silver or whitish; the flowers can be made into a tea. Native Area: Western Europe; throughout North America and northern Eurasia. Medicinal part: Flowers (usually dried) & leaves, root. Medicinal uses Diuretic (kidney), expectorant, nervine (nervous system), sedative, tonic, vermifuge (expels worms).

- **Skullcap**

This herb is often used for the same reasons as skullcap, but it brings relief from pain in headaches. It can also be consumed for treating anxiety and depression and digestive issues such as diarrhea or gas. It can also be applied topically for cuts, scrapes, or other skin conditions such as burns, eczema, or psoriasis.

- **Slippery Elm**

It helps relieve pain and inflammation in the body by reducing swelling and inflammation in the joints and muscles and reducing fever. It can also be boiled with other herbs to promote healthy liver functions, such as replacing damaged tissue and upgrading a healthy mind and body.

- **Star Anise**

Helps with digestion, coughing, and respiratory issues. It is often used in seasoning dishes and contains phytoactive compounds said to help with blood pressure, cholesterol, and weight loss.

- **Stinging Nettle**

It can also be boiled with other herbs to help with indigestion, abdominal cramping, or nausea.

- **Sulfur**

This herb is used to make a soothing poultice for cuts, rashes, and burns while also having strong disinfectant properties and treating many infections. It can also be boiled with other herbs for promoting healthy digestion, such as gas or nausea.

- **Sweet Woodruff**

The part of the plant used/Medicinal part: Leaves. Medicinal uses Analgesic (pain reliever), anti-tussive (cough suppressor), anti-inflammatory, carminative (gas), diuretic (kidney), expectorant, stimulant (circulatory effects).

- **Thyme**

This herb comes in a tea form that helps relieve pain in various situations such as joint aches, headaches, tension headaches, or more. It can also be boiled with other herbs for promoting digestion, such as gas or nausea. Thyme oil can also be applied topically for cuts, scrapes, or different skin conditions such as burns.

Thyme has an attractive scent and taste that is often used in French cuisine for cooking meats such as beef, pork, or lamb.

- **Turmeric**

This herb is commonly used in Indian cooking for enhancing the flavor of foods, but it also has many other uses, such as helping with pain due to arthritis or sprains or bruises. It can be consumed or applied topically on skin conditions such as acne, eczema, psoriasis, or dermatitis. It can also be boiled with other herbs for various things, including digestive issues such as gas, indigestion, diarrhea, or nausea.

- **Uva Ursi**

It helps with reducing inflammation throughout the body. It can also be boiled with other herbs to help with indigestion, abdominal cramping, or nausea.

- **Vanilla Beans**

It helps with many uses, including pain control, stress, and anxiety. It can also be boiled with other herbs for promoting restful sleep during the night by reducing inflammation throughout the body.

- **Verbena**

This herb is often used for stomach cramps, gas, diarrhea, or nausea. It can also be boiled with other herbs to relieve pain caused by anything from rheumatism to arthritis.

- **Violet**

This herb is commonly used in teas to help with stomach cramps, menstrual cramps, and coughs. It can also be applied topically for cuts, scrapes, or other types of skin conditions.

- **Violet Leaf**

This herb comes in a tea form with many uses, including helping with pain control, stress, and anxiety and helping to promote restful sleep during the night. It can also be boiled with other herbs to help with indigestion, abdominal cramping, or nausea.

- **Walnut**

This herb is used to make a soothing poultice for cuts, rashes, and burns while also having strong disinfectant properties and treating many infections. It can also be boiled with other herbs for promoting healthy liver functions, such as replacing damaged tissue.

- **Watercress**

This herb has many uses, including helping to prevent iron deficiency due to its high content of iron and calcium. In contrast, it helps with digestion as well as urinary tract issues. It can be consumed or applied topically depending on the condition being treated.

- **White Willow Bark**

This herb is often used to help reduce inflammation in the body because it contains salicylates that can help those with arthritis, sore muscles, or other afflictions. It can also be boiled with other herbs to treat backaches, headaches, nausea, and stomach cramps.

- **Witch Hazel**

This herb is often used for sore muscles and joints as well as a hemorrhoid treatment. It has been used topically for cuts, scrapes, or other types of skin conditions. The leaves of this plant are also placed on wounds to stop bleeding while helping to relieve pain.

- **Wormwood**

Helps with stomach cramps, gas, and diarrhea. It also has been used topically to treat skin conditions such as acne, eczema, psoriasis, and dermatitis. It can be consumed or boiled with other herbs depending on the condition being treated.

The dried leaves have been used as medicine. Native Area: Western Europe; throughout North America and northern Eurasia. Medicinal part: Leaves. Medicinal uses Antirheumatic (prevents stiffness and inflammation), antispasmodic, aperitif (eases digestion), antiseptic (topical, internal), cholagogue, depurative (a liver stimulant), diaphoretic (promotes perspiration), emmenagogue, expectorant (promotes secretion of mucus in the respiratory tract to help clear the airways in a cough), febrifuge (reduces fever), hepatic (stimulates the liver to remove toxins from blood - used for jaundice and hepatitis.), nervine(calms the nerves, reduces stress and fear).

- **Yarrow**

This herb is often used for treating bleeding cuts or wounds because it has a coagulating effect while helping with fevers and dizziness. It can also be boiled with other herbs to help with various things, including indigestion, menstrual cramps, and colds or flu symptoms.

Yarrow oil can also be applied topically for cuts, scrapes, or other types of skin conditions such as burns.

- **Yellow Dock**

It is a perennial herb with stalky branching stems and grass-like leaves. The flowers are yellow, and the seeds are red and round. Native Area: Widespread throughout Europe, North America, and Asia; cultivated in many other countries.

This herb has many uses, including gonorrhea, menstrual cramps, ulcers, and more. It can also be boiled with other herbs for treating stomach aches and diarrhea.

- **Wild Yam**

A perennial vine native to North America is found in dry woods, open fields, and prairies. The root is used to make medicine. It can also be found in cultivated gardens.

Native Areas: Eastern America: Eastern Canada and the Eastern United States.

The part of the plant used/Medicinal part: Root

Medicinal uses: Antirheumatic, antispasmodic, antiseptic, cholagogue, diaphoretic, diuretic (liver), emetic (strong), expectorant, laxative(strong), purgative (strong), stimulant(blood).

Globulin (a constituent of yam) is a potent agent against the "Herpes Simplex" 2 virus - the virus that causes genital herpes.

CHAPTER 9:

Various Types of Fasting

With various methods of intermittent fasting available, there is bound to be a method that suits your lifestyle. Some approaches are more intense than others, and it is to be noted that the fasts that yield more radical results are generally those that require more radical dedication. However, even small fasts can boost your metabolism and help you see results. Some methods, like the 5:2 diet, do not require a full fast, but rather a large decrease in the number of calories consumed on fast days. The 16:8 diet simply involves skipping one meal a day. These two methods are generally considered the least daunting and are good ways to introduce your body to fasting. Other methods include the "eat - stop – eat" diet (which involves a 24-hour fast once or twice each week), alternate day fasting, and the warrior diet. Which method you choose depends on various factors like your schedule, special events, responsibilities to feed others, biology, weight loss or muscle gain goals, and workout routine. Whatever needs you have to meet, there is a method of intermittent fasting that can suit your life.

Water Fasting

The first type of fasting we will look at is water fasting. Water fasting is a method of fasting in which a person does not ingest anything except water for a period of time. Many people practice water fasting for periods up to 72 hours, but this is a decision that should be made with the help of a doctor.

If you have ever gone into the hospital for a medical procedure, they likely told you that you could not eat food and could only drink water for a certain amount of time before the procedure. This practice would have been a form of water fasting. Some people also try water fasting as a method of "detoxing" their bodies. Another use for it is to manually induce autophagy. Many people practice periods of water fasting to induce autophagy in order to rid their bodies of potentially harmful viruses or bacteria in an effort to reduce their risk of diseases such as cancer and Alzheimer's and even increase their lifespan. This is because of the cleansing properties of autophagy, as it breaks down infected cells and uses their salvageable parts for new and healthy cells to be generated. Autophagy can reduce the risk of cancers because of the way it clears the body of damaged cells, which could otherwise accumulate and develop into cancer.

There are added benefits of water fasting that do not directly involve autophagy, but that is worth noting anyway. It has been shown to reduce blood pressure, cholesterol and even improve the functioning of insulin in the body, therefore improving blood sugar.

The problem with water fasting is that it can be quite dangerous if not practiced in a safe and monitored way. Consult a doctor before attempting a water fast so that you can ensure you are doing so in a safe way. Some groups of people should not practice water fasting. These include pregnant women, children, the elderly, and people with eating disorders.

Another warning to keep in mind when attempting a water fast in an effort to lose weight is that the weight lost during a water fast may not be the exact type of weight you are trying to lose. During a water fast, there is a severe restriction in calories, which leads to the breakdown of fat stores, but some of the weight loss could also include water weight, stored carbohydrates and sometimes muscle (in longer fasts). What this means is that after a water fast, the weight loss may come back quite quickly if the majority was water or carbohydrate stores, as these are replenished very quickly once a person begins eating again. If this is the case, do not be concerned, this is a very normal reaction for your body to have as it is built to anticipate unexpected fasts and therefore has ways to protect you from these, such as storing carbohydrates.

When approaching a water fast, it is beneficial to prepare your body for a few days leading up to it by tapering off your eating portions in order to gradually remove food from your day. This will better prepare your body to go without food for a day or two. Another way to get your body prepared to water fast is to fast for part of the day so that it can get accustomed to spending some time without food. You may also be wondering how a water fast could make you lose water weight, but it is entirely possible and even likely. This is because much of the water we bring into our bodies throughout the day is enclosed in the foods we eat. If your water intake remains the same, but your food ingestion dramatically decreases, you could end up becoming dehydrated and thus losing water weight. You will also need to adjust your activities to accommodate this water fast, especially if it is your first time trying it. If you are not used to fasting, you may feel dizzy or light-headed, and this may make some of your daily tasks more difficult. This could be due to lower blood sugar or lower blood pressure if you are dehydrated. Be sure to keep this in mind as you attempt a water fast and be sure to increase your water intake to avoid a drop in blood pressure. There is still much more research that needs to be done surrounding water fasting in humans in particular. Water fasting as a method of weight loss is a relatively new approach and one that is just beginning to be explored with human test subjects.

One Meal a Day

One of the most extreme fasting methods, the OMAD (one meal a day) diet requires you to eat— as per its name—only one meal a day, for just one hour, which means fasting for the other 23 hours. This is an intense form of intermittent fasting, and as such, it is not advised as your introductory step into the fasting practice.

A softer way to approach this diet is to have a normal meal (many prefer an evening or late afternoon meal) accompanied by 2 very light snacks distanced by 2 hours after or before your daily meal.

The calorie deficit leads to a weight loss but it may also assist in the reduction of some cardiovascular disease risk factors. However, being it the most hardcore type of fasting it is normal to feel the pangs of hunger so one of the most critical points to keep under control is to not let your craving lead to overeating during your meal.

If you do a great number of exercises and training in your days, this is probably not the dietitian regimen I would suggest you, but if you're looking for a kind of fasting that brings results quick and you are willing to extend it for short periods, it is definitely a kind of intermittent fasting you should consider.

What Is One Meal a Day?

One meal a day is the fast track to weight loss and many studies have confirmed that. It also happens to be a good way to live a healthy lifestyle. It helps you keep your calories down while at the same time losing weight faster than if you were eating three meals per day. This type of dieting should only be done until you reach your goal weight, but for some people, this can last for life.

To be able to do this type of dieting, you need to eat a lot of protein. This will keep your body from feeling hungry as quickly. However, you also need to make sure you are eating the right kinds of protein. Lean meats and fish are best for this kind of eating plan. They should be cooked lightly and in a healthy manner, without adding fats or oils that would slow down weight loss.

You should also consider the number of calories you burn during the day. You obviously burn calories when you exercise, but there are other activities that will burn calories as well. For instance, walking around town can burn about 100 calories per hour if you do it regularly. Having an active lifestyle will also help you to lose weight. This is why many people using OMAD find it works really well.

Your daily allowance should be somewhere between 1,000 and 1,500 calories a day. This should help you lose weight quickly without taking the joy out of eating. In addition to this, keep in mind that if you do not eat enough calories, your body will go into the same type of hibernation that it does during sleep. As such, you need to make sure you are eating enough carbohydrates and proteins so it does not go into this mode. A good way to get the right amount of calories is to eat three meals a day, but cut your portions in half. If you do not like the idea of cutting your portions in half, you should try eating just one meal at night.

Benefits of One Meal a Day

Some people will tell you that eating only once a day will keep you from becoming hungry. However, that is not really true for most people. Once your body gets used to this type of dieting, it will feel hungry less often and faster when it does feel hunger. You simply have to give your body time to adjust and then it will work just fine as long as you are taking in enough protein.

Another benefit to eating this way is that it is much easier to stop eating once you are full. Many people find that after they have eaten fewer calories for a while, they stop feeling hungry in the middle of a meal. This makes it easy to eat less and lose weight. It also keeps you from getting too full when you are eating an actual meal with family or friends.

You will also be more aware of what your body is telling you because your stomach will tell you when it is time to eat again. This is a much better way to lose weight than trying to get your body used to smaller portions.

OMAD is ideal for women over 50 who need to lose weight quickly before hitting that big birthday. If you are trying to lose 50 pounds in a year, one meal a day is the fastest way to do it without starving yourself or doing an extreme diet. Just remember that it is not a permanent way of eating. Once you have reached your goal weight, shift back to a normal eating schedule with three meals per day. This will ensure you stay healthy and keep the weight off long-term.

Sure, OMAD fasting may be an odd way of eating, but when it comes down to it, it is not a bad way. Eat a lot of protein, keep your calories down, and you will see yourself losing weight quickly. It is also a nice change of pace from the daily grind.

The 16/8 Method

This involves fasting for a total period of 16 hours in the 24 hours that makes a day.

This method requires a daily fast of 14 hours for women and 16 hours for men. You'll have to limit the times you eat to a total of 8- to 10-hour eating window. With this method, you can incorporate 2 to 3 or more meals in a day.

Martin Berkhan, the famous fitness expert, made this method popular. Some refer to it as the Leangains protocol. It is the most widely known because it is almost natural. The hours you skip meals fall under the time you are either sleeping or working. Most people who skip their breakfast and finish dinner before eight are actually doing the 16-hour protocol, but they don't know that.

Women are instructed to fast for 14 to 15 hours because most do better with this short-range, and during the fast, you have to eat healthy foods during the eating window. The results you want to achieve won't be forthcoming if there's a lot of junk in your food.

You can take water and coffee during the fasting hours as well as other drinks that are no caloric.

To fast with this method, your last meal should be by 8 p.m. while your first meal should be by 12 p.m.

This simple method works because obviously you eat less calories when you are not eating as much as you are used to. Plus, the 16-hour fasting covers your sleeping hours. Unless you dream about eating, 7 or 8 hours of you 16 are going to pass effortlessly. Your body is working for you while you sleep! If you can do it, you could even think about extending your sleeping time to get you closer to your eating window.

Changing your eating habits may be tough but this kind of fasting process is easy and flexible enough for you to start your journey with the right foot.

Benefits of 16/8 Method

Intermittent fasting has numerous benefits. The 16/8 method, in particular, has a lot of advantages in addition to being the simplest, safest, and the most doable method of all the different intermittent fasting methods. Let's see a few of these benefits below.

Fat Burn/Weight Loss

One of the biggest advantages of any intermittent fasting technique is the assurance of weight loss through the fat burn. No other diets that promise weight loss can deliver with such an assurance for a long and permanent duration. Because intermittent fasting is a lifestyle change and not a random diet restriction, this should assure you the fat burn is long-lasting and permanent.

This is a guaranteed result because the science behind it is flawless and anyone practicing intermittent fasting will see the results of being in an extended fasted state are efficient weight loss and fat burn. When the body's immediate reserves of glucose are depleted, it moves on to ready to use glucose stored as glycogen. When these are exhausted, the body moves on to consuming the fat stores to produce energy. This fat-burning process is known as ketosis, and it produces ketones, which are a signal of the fat-burning process. A body in a prolonged fasting state shows the presence of ketones in the bloodstream, which means the body is actively burning fats. This is a sign to rejoice because the stored fats are at last getting burned. This is what causes weight loss. With any intermittent fasting technique, this is a foolproof process. Though the time of ketosis varies from one method to another based on the number of hours the body spends fasting, all methods have a fat-burning period.

Blood Sugar Regulation

Intermittent fasting also helps regulate the levels of glucose in the blood. As insulin levels gradually decrease as the body moves into the fasting state, the levels of glucose in the bloodstream have already been taken care of. In the fasting state, there is no food, so no insulin and no new glucose is produced. This fasting state gives time to the body to adjust its responses to food and glucose production, with appropriate insulin release in the feeding state. A person with a normal eating schedule eats several meals, big and small, with numerous snacks throughout the day. This means there is always some amount of glucose present in the bloodstream, and several insulin spikes as the day goes on. This is effectively dealt with by fasting.

Boosts Focus and Cognition

Intermittent fasting helps boost brain function. It gives us a special type of mental clarity and improves focus. This happens because a simple 16-hour fast pushes our body into the ketosis process where the body produces ketones and breaks them down to generate energy in place of glucose. It has been known that when the brain uses ketones for energy instead of glucose it gives a boost to the brain's functionality. Also, the hunger hormone ghrelin undergoes a lot of changes during the fasting period. This positively influences the levels of dopamine, which is a neurotransmitter essential for mental clarity and lucid brain function. This is why fasting is said to have a positive effect on how well our brain functions. Our concentration, focus, and cognition is seen to improve by leaps and bounds through intermittent fasting.

Body Cleansing and Longevity

Studies have shown that switching from glucose-driven energy processes to ketone-based energy processes causes the body to remain in a cleansing state. The body, when in a fasting period, moves to heal, rectify, restore, and replenish several of its broken and damaged tissues. This helps the body to remain healthy for longer durations. This cleansing also helps remove harmful substances from the body like toxins, waste and broken cells. Also, intermittent fasting has been shown to have several positive effects on keeping diseases at bay, including cancer and Alzheimers.

Stress Resistance

Intermittent fasting also increases our body's resistance to stress of different kinds. Here again, the process of ketosis plays a part. Our body produces a stress-induced hormone known as cortisol, which is necessary to have balanced and low levels of this hormone. Intermittent fasting for longer durations of time with longer fasting periods increases the levels of cortisol in our body and induces greater stress. But, intermittent fasting with gradually increasing fasting periods can actually help regulate cortisol levels and keep stress at bay. This is especially true in the case of the 16/8 method as this has a shorter fasting period compared to other more complex techniques. Methods like OMAD or one meal a day and alternate fasting with twenty-four-hour fasting periods can actually increase stress levels with increased cortisol levels. The opposite is true with the 16/8 method.

Drawbacks of 16/8 Method

One of the biggest drawbacks of this method of intermittent fasting is the shorter fat-burning period. In a typical sixteen-hour fast, the body begins the process of ketosis by the thirteenth hour. So, for a sixteen-hour fast, your body only has three hours to burn fat. Three hours of ketosis results in mild fat consumption. This process occurs at the liver where ketones are produced and is helpful for those suffering from the effects of a fatty liver. Three hours can seem like a short time to effectively carry out the process, but this can be corrected by pushing the body into ketosis quicker.

The 5:2 Diet

British journalist Michael Mosley popularized this method. It has also been called the fast diet.

This method requires that you limit the number of calories you consume to only 500 for females and 600 for males two days a week. That means you usually eat for five days and reduce the calories in your diet for two days.

For example, you might eat every day of the week except Tuesday and Thursday, when you reduce the food you consume. You limit the calories for breakfast to 250 for women and 300 for men, while dinner takes the same number of calories as well.

This is similar to the Eat-Stop-Eat method, except that instead of fully fasting on Monday and Thursday (for example), you will greatly restrict your caloric intake. For the other five days of the week, you will eat as you normally would. This is a method of intermittent eating, though it does not involve complete fasting. This method would be good for those who are unable to completely fast for two days of the week but who want to try a form of intermittent eating still. For example, this would be a good option for someone who works a physically laborious job and who cannot be feeling light-headed during the workday.

Every diet has a few downsides, and some people will struggle more than others. The fact that the 5:2 diet does not require a full fast from calories can actually make it a bit harder to get used to. Meeting a small calorie count rather than avoiding food altogether can leave one feeling hungrier and more focused on the lack of food. Fasting from food in its entirety affects the production of hunger hormones, and over time your body will start to get less hungry during your fasting periods. When you are restricting calories dramatically but still eating, this change in hormones does not occur. You may be left feeling the effects of your hunger much more than someone who chooses another fasting routine. During other methods of fasting, it can also help to distract yourself from the food you are not eating. The 5:2 diet does not allow this quite as much. In fact, if you are serious about your weight loss goals and desire to make the most of your minuscule calorie allotment for the day, you may find you are even more focused on food than normal. It's also important to note that your fast days should be scheduled on days when you won't be over-exerting yourself. Because you are giving yourself less fuel, intense workouts or high levels of physical exertion will be difficult on the body. Yoga and light exercise like walking may be ideal for the two days during which your calorie count is low.

Why it works: By relying on just two days of calorie reduction, you put yourself in a spot to lose weight while still getting more comfortable when you get to eat something on those two days.

The catch: Well, the first time you try to adjust your eating habits you'll cut your calories a lot, which will take some planning and some deep breaths. It may not be easy at first, but hey, who wants it easy? On top of that, you do have to eat healthy on the other five days. I would advise against eating pizza and burgers for five days and lettuce and lemon wedges the next two.

Eat-Stop-Eat

This method requires you to do a 24-hour fast either once or twice a week, whichever one is comfortable for you.

An example is not eating from 7 p.m. to 7 p.m. the next day. That is, if you start with dinner on Monday, you don't eat from 7 p.m. Monday to 7 p.m. Tuesday. You can do this once or twice a week. If it is once, it is advisable for it to be done mid-week, like Wednesday, and if it is twice, it is good if the days are spread apart, e.g., Monday and Thursday.

You can drink water, coffee, and other no caloric drinks between fasting periods, but solid foods are not allowed. It is, however, not advisable to start with this method as it requires a lot of energy for long hours without food. Start with 16 hours fasting before plunging into the 24 hours fast.

In the days of the week in which you do not fast, you are allowed to eat normally, but once again, this means following a healthy regular eating schedule and not binging as an answer to a quick feeding desire fulfillment.

If you want to add some (fairly serious) exercise in order to boost the weight loss benefit, I suggest you increase by 20% the calories intake the other nonfasting days. Adding exercise (and yoga!) is also a way to make the process simpler and more manageable while you are having a calorie deficit.

Also during this diet, you may control hunger during fasting days by drinking water, tea or coffee. This is the perfect fasting method for those who want to put together the fasting effort in just one or two days and then forget about it. I suggest getting on these fasting 2 days a week.

Alternate-day Fasting

Most of the health benefits revealed are as a result of this method, fasting on alternate days.

There are two variations to this method;

a) 24-hour full day fasting every other day. This requires you to eat normally for a day and then fast for the next 24 hours.
b) Eating only a few hundred calories. The alternate-day fasting can be very challenging, and this made the experts devise another plan where you only eat a reduced number of calories every other day.

An example is that when you fast on Monday, you eat normally on Tuesday, fast on Wednesday, and continue for the rest of the week.

Pros of Alternate Day Fast

- A natural way to lose weight. The idea is that by alternating between feast and famine you will be able to lose weight while your body is in a calorie deficit state.
- Less hunger than traditional diets - hunger is known to be one of the main reasons why people quit their diet plans. With ADF you'll end up experiencing less hunger pangs than on a regular diet, which makes it easier for you to stay on track.
- Based on scientific research—I know, strange as it sounds.

This is a good thing for several reasons.

As we've established already, your body needs at least 12 hours to process food and get ready for the next meal. So, if you eat breakfast at 8:00 am today, you'll be hungry before bedtime and will need to eat a substantial snack in order to sleep until morning. That's not ideal.

Intermittent fasting (which is what ADF is) has been scientifically proven to raise human growth hormone levels. This is a key element in building lean muscle mass, decreasing body fat levels and improving overall health.

When following ADF your insulin levels will be much more stable (insulin spikes are one of the main reasons for weight gain/obesity). It also makes it easier to lose weight, because when you're eating less regularly, insulin sensitivity increases as well.

However, this isn't a 'magic' solution— it's just another tool you can use in your arsenal against obesity and related health problems.

A word of caution: If you're going to try ADF, don't expect it to be a walk in the park. Since your body goes into short periods of famine when following this diet, it's bound to cause some hunger and cravings. It might also give you headaches, mood swings and other side effects—but these are temporary!

ADF is best for women, post-menopausal women, the elderly and anyone with medical issues. If you're young and physically active, you probably won't benefit from following ADF.

Below Are Descriptions of The Most Popular Alternative Day Fasting Diets:

- **QOD Diet**

The QOD Diet is a diet program based on a book that is all about on days and off days. On your "On Days" you are allowed to eat fairly regularly, but you must watch your sodium and potassium intake. On your "Off Days," you are relegated to eat only 500 calories and only 200 of them are allowed to come from protein. Again you are asked to limit sodium and potassium.

On top of that, you are asked to take supplements and protein powders to help regulate what you ingest. This will help facilitate faster weight loss according to the creators of this alternate day diet plan.

- **Up Day Down Day Diet**

This diet takes the QOD Diet a little farther because it does not require using so many supplements and potions to help with weight loss. It starts with the induction phase where you are on "Up Days and Down Days" (sounds familiar right?). During induction, you will be restricted to 500 calories and you are not as constrained by sodium and potassium. This makes the diet a little easier than the QOD. On down days you are allowed to eat regularly as long as you don't "purposely overeat"

That last statement is a little more ambiguous when you are starving yourself the day before.

After the induction phase, you go to the maintenance phase, where your down days are eating 50% of your normal eating routine.

- **The Every Other Day Diet (EODD)**

The EODD goes even further towards the ultimate alternate day diet. The EODD has different phases like the Up Day Down Day Diet, but they work the same in each phase. The reason this diet is more refined is that it incorporates the SNAPP Eating Plan which tells you exactly what to eat. So on "Burn" days, you eat exactly what the SNAPP Plan tells you.

On "Feed" days you can eat pizza, hamburgers etc. as long as it is during the times outlined in SNAPP. The rest of the meals you eat what's told in the plan.

- **The Warrior Diet**

This method of fasting was made famous by Ori Hofmekler, another fitness expert.

This diet requires you to fast or eat a small or little chunk of food during the day while consuming a huge meal at night, a typical case of fast and feast later. You eat small amounts of fruits and vegetables during the day and fall back to a huge meal.

The meal is best eaten by 4 p.m. in the evening. No food must be eaten until the next morning, when you continue with fruits and vegetables.

A feast for dinner and fast for the day.

The Warrior Diet was created by an ex-member of the Israeli Special Forces, who found inspiration in his time as a soldier and carried his knowledge and experience into the field of fitness and nutrition. However, the creator of this diet admits that it is not based on science and the amount of research around it is nearly non-existent. This does not necessarily mean it isn't effective, but it is a good point to remember when considering this method.

Many people who practice the Warrior Diet incorporate exercise into their routine during the fasting period. This can be an effective way to build muscle, but it carries potentially harmful side effects. Pushing the body to its limits when it is low on fuel (food) can cause fatigue and dehydration, as well as decreasing your overall ability to perform, which may lead to injury. This can also lead to a condition called hypoglycemia, which is essentially dangerously low blood sugar. Hypoglycemia can lead to problems of varying severities ranging from confusion, increased clumsiness, trouble forming words, and dizziness to seizures and possible death. If you have type 1 diabetes or are on medication designed to lower your blood sugar, you should never attempt this diet. Again, it is important to consult your doctor before trying to incorporate a fasting regime into your lifestyle. An extended fast such as this also increases the likelihood of binge eating and consuming foods that are not rich in the nutrients necessary to fuel the body. When you are consuming a full day's worth of calories in 4 hours, opting for a carb-heavy meal full of processed food may seem appealing. Ensuring your body is receiving the proper vitamins and minerals to maintain its functions is crucial to a healthy practice of intermittent fasting. Incorporating a meal prep plan into your Warrior Diet can help to avoid this issue and increase your likelihood of success.

Practicing any method of intermittent fasting is not recommended for people who may suffer from eating disorders. Any restrictive diet is not suggested for people with a tendency to over-restrict calories. Also, most people do not use intermittent fasting as a lifelong commitment, so someday they will probably stop practicing it. After you become accustomed to fasting, eating on a normal schedule can cause unwanted weight gain. You may lose touch with your ability to sense when you are truly hungry or full, and you may become accustomed to eating higher-calorie meals. If you are not careful, this may lead to overeating, which can bring about feelings of shame or regret that can negatively affect mental health. In individuals who are at risk of disordered eating, the negative emotions connected to this can lead to bingeing and purging behaviors.

Depending on the state of your health, your lifestyle, your weight loss or muscle gain goals, and your reaction to fasting, there is likely a method of intermittent fasting that suits your needs. The 5:2 diet and time-restricted eating methods like the 16:8 are ideal for beginners and have much fewer risks attached. If you want fast, drastic results, the Warrior Diet may be ideal for you. All of these methods will help you lose fat. Some will help you lose more fat, more quickly, and some will help you build and maintain muscle mass more effectively. You do not have to stick to one method forever. The beauty of fasting is that it can be done in whatever way suits your lifestyle the best and can be catered individually to your wants and desires.

With such original claims, it's no wonder this approach has not yet sufficient scientific data to back it up. But even though there is no clear study on the Warrior Diet, it is a diet which is getting more and more popular, with its giving room for some food during its fasting window. Even if a bit impractical, given the requirement of eating at night, its popularity is rising, especially among gym lovers. The period in which you are allowed to the greater amount of food is reduced; during this period the diet makes large use of paleo foods. Being the fasting time a 20 hours' period, it is stricter than other types of intermittent fasting.

This diet, like other intermittent fasting strategies, can lead to weight loss when a caloric deficit is reached.

How Does It Work and Why is it Beneficial?

This diet works because of how your nervous system is set up to handle the digestion of food and funnelling of available energy. During the 20 hours when you are under eating, the Sympathetic Nervous System (SNS) is responsible for your ability to deal with stress, physical activity and periods of intense concentration. Basically anytime you need energy or cohesive body function, it is the responsibility of the SNS to provide you with it. Whenever you eat, the SNS gets turned off as the parasympathetic nervous system (PNS) gets turned on, which is responsible for the digestion of food. This is why after having a big lunch it is common to have energy crashes and feel like taking a nap as opposed to carrying on with the day. Taking a nap anytime you eat a meal or a snack does sound nice, but who in this day and age has the time for that?

The overeating phase of the Warrior Diet will typically be during 4 hours of the evening. The PNS will be maximized during this time and will aid in resting, digestion and detoxification, among other things. All food groups will need to be consumed during this period of time; however, it does not mean that you should binge on junk food and sugary snacks. Usually, this will not be a problem because a person on this diet will crave the foods that the body actually needs as opposed to the foods that one might crave if they wanted to indulge their taste buds only. Of course, during the first few weeks or even months, there will be a transition period where you will need to condition yourself to lose the cravings for your old eating habits. This can be particularly difficult if you have a strong reliance on sugary foods and drinks. It has been said that a person's desire for food is the hardest to suppress, so this diet really does put this statement to the test.

- **Spontaneous Meal Skipping**

This is a more natural method than the 16/8 because there's no routine. You just skip meals when convenient.

This can be done in some instances, such as when you are not really hungry or are on a journey and can't find suitable food to eat. You can skip these meals.

There's no routine to this method. You can decide to skip your meal anytime, from lunch to dinner to breakfast. Once you don't follow a routine, you are using this method.

These methods, however, are not suitable for every individual, and you don't need to try everything before you know which is ideal for you.

This guide is for women over 50 years old, and this kind of people often lose energy more rapidly than typical younger youths so methods, such as the alternate-day fasting and the eat-stop-eat method, are not suitable for women over fifty because these types and processes require a lot of energy, which these women lack.

The 16/8 is not suitable for every one woman over fifty, but it's a good start if you want to take the fast to another level. There's no magic to it, and no one can tell you what's best for you. You have to discover yourself.

The spontaneous meal skipping is a great place to start, but the results won't be as fast as the other methods because of the lack of routine.

The best methods, however, are the eat-stop-eat and the 5:2. These two have routines you can follow, but you don't need to stay away from food, only consume small calories. This way, you fast with a routine, and the results will be achieved.

Whichever you decide to use, make sure you consult your doctor to see if intermittent fasting is suitable for you.

The method had been popularized by Krista Varady, PhD, a nutrition professor at the University of Illinois in Chicago. According to this plan, fasters are allowed to 25% of their daily calorie requirements (which are approximately 500 calories), while nonfasting days can be regular eating days. This is a very common weight-loss technique. Dr. Varady and colleagues observed in a small study published in Nutrition Journal that alternate-day fasting was successful in helping obese adults lose weight. By week two, the side effects (such as hunger) diminished and the participants continued to become more comfortable with the diet by week four.

The calories on fasting days must be consumed with one meal of your preference, lunch or dinner.

A useful help for achieving results with this dietary regimen is constituted by fluids: drink a lot of water, tea (or herbal tea) and unsweetened coffee.

It is important to note that if you wish to incorporate physically demanding exercise into your day, you should be aware of how your body reacts to working out in a fasted state versus a fed state and schedule your meals and workouts accordingly. Some people choose to do fasted workouts for a variety of reasons, and some find that their bodies are simply not adequately fueled for such workouts during the fasting period. Your fasting method should be adapted to suit your life, so pay attention to your body and take it into consideration. Pushing your body to work out when you have less energy due to fasting can lead to ineffective workouts and even injury. Many sports nutritionists advise choosing a fasting schedule that coincides with your ideal workout schedule so you can fuel your body immediately before or after exercise. If you are practicing the 16:8 methods by skipping breakfast, this may mean working out in the afternoon or evening. Many people prefer to work out in the morning when human growth hormone levels are naturally highest. If this is the case for you, you may choose to implement your feeding window in the morning and begin your fast in the afternoon rather than the evening.

Time-Restricted Fasting

This kind of fasting is also referred to as "time-restricted eating."

See it like an introductory road to heavier forms of fasting. It simply requires you to choose an eating window which will need to be respected each day. The typical eating window ranges from 6 to 12 hours a day. As the most attentive would have noticed, this is just a more flexible 16:8 fasting program. Maybe you would be more comfortable with 12-hour fasting, which is very similar to a regular day eating cycle. What changes here though is your mindset: too easy? Great! Do it in the right way then; eat only healthy food without snacking around. This program is an excellent way to "rest" in between different fasting methods or fasting periods.

Also, this kind of fasting encourages autophagy and general health. You would be surprised about how many benefits your body will register just by sticking to your guns and show yourself discipline in peaceful times.

For example, set your meal window from 9 a.m. to 6 p. m. and be consistent to respect this window. This works really nicely with those of us who are very busy tending to our families or taking care of the house and have to follow a fixed routine. Lay down your simple plan and be consistent!

Fasting Mimicking Diet

Fast mimicking is a type of modified fasting. Instead of abstaining from food completely like a traditional fast, you still consume small amounts of food in a way that produces the therapeutic benefits of fasting.

A fast mimicking diet typically lasts about five days and follows a healthy protocol low in carbs, protein, and calories and high in fat. Calories are kept at around 40% of normal intake. This allows the body to stay nourished with nutrients and electrolytes, and will give you less stress than normal fasting but while still receiving the same benefits.

Long-term calorie restriction and long-term fasting may be harmful, but fast mimicking is safer and more effective. Let's look at how much it differs from traditional fasting.

According to the advice of the World Health Organization, consuming these five a day portions will assist any average person in reducing their risks of suffering heart disease, a stroke or a variety of cancers. The diet that includes these portions will also likely reduce the problems of diabetes and obesity, by helping to reduce artificial sugars in the diet and reducing our propensity in Western cultures to eat too much, which is what has led to the obesity epidemic all around us.

You eat 500-1000 calories a day for 2-5 days and on day 6 you return to a normal way of eating. It can be used for weight loss, fighting disease, and promoting longevity. Here's how it works:

- You eat about 500-1000 calories every day.
- Your daily macros are low protein, moderate carb, moderate fat.
- You eat foods like a nutbar, a bowl of soup, and some crackers with a few olives or something.
- Day One you eat about 1000 calories – 10% protein, 55% fat, and 35% carbs.
- Day 2-5 you eat about 500-700 calories – 10% protein, 45% fat, 45% carbs.
- Day 6 you transition back to a normal caloric intake with complex carbs, vegetables, and minimal meat, fish, and cheese.

Protein Sparing Modified Fasting

The idea of a PSMF is to reduce calories to the lowest possible threshold while still eating enough protein to preserve lean tissue mass and enough micronutrients to avoid deficiency. This is basically a kind of starvation, so you get the same metabolic benefits that you do with a "real" fast (which is also basically a kind of starvation), but the additional protein and nutrients make the whole project a little less risky and minimize muscle loss and potential nutrient deficiencies.

Practically, a PSMF involves:

Very few calories (typically under 1,000 per day – remember that the point is to induce a starvation response), with the vast majority coming from lean protein. Fat and carbs are minimized as much as possible.

A few non-starchy vegetables.

Supplemental vitamins, minerals, and salts to make up the inevitable nutrient and electrolyte deficiencies.

On a PSMF, the majority of calories entering your mouth are from protein, but the majority of calories you burn for energy come from fat; patients on a PSMF do go into ketosis. That's because you can't "burn" protein for energy the way you burn fat or carbs. The protein is just there to replenish muscle mass and prevent lean tissue loss – it's used as building blocks, not as fuel. Instead of burning that protein for fuel, you'll be burning your own body fat reserves; so, you essentially are "eating" fat – your own fat.

A PSMF consists of two phases. The first "intensive" phase lasts 4-6 months and involves severely limiting calories.

The second "refeeding" phase lasts 6-8 weeks, during which calories are gradually increased back to a more regular level.

Fat Fasting

A fat fast is a high-fat, low-calorie diet that typically lasts 2–5 days.

During this time it's recommended to eat 1,000–1,200 calories per day, 80–90% of which should come from fat.

Though not technically a fast, this approach mimics the biological effects of abstaining from food by putting your body into the biological state of ketosis.

In ketosis your body uses fat, rather than carbs, as its main energy source. During this process, your liver breaks down fatty acids into molecules called ketones, which can be used to fuel your body.

Ketosis occurs during times when glucose, your body's main source of energy, isn't available, such as during periods of starvation or when your carb intake is very low.

The time it takes to achieve ketosis can vary considerably, but if you're following a ketogenic diet, you can typically expect to reach this state between days 2 and 6.

Fat fasting is designed to get you into ketosis quickly or to boost ketone levels if you have already achieved ketosis by restricting both your calorie and carb intake.

It's usually used by people on a ketogenic diet who want to break through an ongoing weight loss plateau or by those wanting to get back into ketosis after a cheat day, on which the rules of a low-carb diet are relaxed and you eat foods that are high in carbs.

A fat fast is very low in calories and high in fat. It's designed to create a calorie deficit, which is needed for weight loss, while quicly depleting your body's carb stores so you move into ketosis and burn more fat.

Thus, if you adhere to this protocol strictly for 2–5 days, you may enter ketosis and begin burning fat as your primary source of fuel, particularly if you're already on a very-low-carb diet.

Nonetheless, a fat fast only last a few days, so large shifts on the scale can't be explained by fat loss alone.

The loss of your body's carb stores also leads to a loss of water, which is stored alongside glycogen, the stored form of glucose. This gives the illusion of fat loss.

Bone Broth Fasting

A bone broth fast means you consume bone broth several times per day but not much other solid food. Fasts are not for everyone, and sometimes certain kinds can pose risks since they involve consuming little nutrients due to greatly reducing calorie intake. However, if you make a good candidate, consuming bone broth is ideal for a fast because it's chock-full of important macronutrients and micronutrients, including amino acids (which form proteins) like glycine, arginine and proline; vitamins and minerals; collagen; electrolytes; and even antioxidants like glucosamine.

Most people do best fasting for a period between three to four days, during this time consuming several quarts of bone broth daily and eliminating many problematic foods. One of the advantages that makes a bone broth fast stand apart from other alternatives, is that it's an ideal way to obtain more collagen, which is a type of protein needed to create healthy tissue found throughout the body. Collagen is found inside the lining of the digestive tract, within bones in bone marrow, in skin, and in the tissues that form joints, tendons, ligaments and cartilage.

Within collagen we find other special nutrients, including amino acids like proline and glycine, plus gelatin; all have widespread benefits.

How to Start a Bone Broth Fast?

Typically the fast lasts anywhere between 24 hours and 3 days, but we recommend starting small if you're new to fasting or consuming a diet high in processed food.

Most bone broth fasts consist of consuming between 3 to 4 quarts of bone broth per day while avoiding solid food and intense exercise. Fasting allows your body to burn fat, boost your metabolism, and heal conditions such as leaky gut due to its ability to restore good bacteria in the digestive tract. When you add in the numerous benefits of bone broth protein, the electrolyte and amino acid content hydrates, these come togeter to detox and heal your body.

Most fasting is done without solid food. However, if you are new to fasting or are feeling light-headed, it's okay to include one small meal of grass-fed meat and vegetables for every 24 hours of fasting.

Dry Fasting

Dry fasting is a type of fast that doesn't allow any water intake. The lack of water may help accelerate some of the protective effects you get on a regular water fast, like reduced inflammation and metabolic health.

However, it's a more advanced fasting method that only people who have previous experience with normal fasts should attempt.

Dry fasting has been perfected and practiced by many cultures and religions throughout history:

- Judaism (during Yom Kippur)
- Christianity (during Lent and Advent)
- Mormonism (one Sunday of each month)
- Buddhism (to aid meditation)
- Jainism (to reach transcendence)
- Islam (during Ramadan)

The Islamic, Mormon, and Jewish fasts are the only ones that prohibit water, so they're true dry fasts.

There Are Two Popular Types Of Dry Fasting Methods

Hard and soft dry fasting is very popular. With the hard dry fast, the faster does not even allow water to touch their body. None!

When dry fasting the pores of the skin absorb water from contact with the environment.

This is one of the reasons many dry fasting experts believe it is best to practice in the outdoors, in the mountains as opposed to in cities.

This much cleaner environment is preferred as the skin absorbs water through the moisture in the air. Sleeping outside and near running water in this environment is ideal for longer dry fasting.

As you can imagine, the soft dry fast allows the participant to drink water during the fast. The presence of water lessens the beneficial and the uncomfortable effects of dry fasting but allows the faster to fast for longer periods of time. This is preferred for beginners.

Juice Fasting

Juice fasting is a great way to get off the dieting rollercoaster and see real results quickly. Safe and effective when carried out correctly, juice fasting benefits your entire being.

Your physical wellbeing increases as the body is rid of toxins and excess fat.

Your mind benefits because fasting creates a stillness that brings mental clarity and helps you to develop will power and to better control your senses.

As you lose weight and feel much better about yourself, self-esteem improves and sets you on the road to what could be a life-changing experience, connecting you to your spirit and helping you to achieve balance in your life.

General Juicing Rules:

- Drink freshly prepared juice and do not store the juice for over 24 hours. If you can't drink it immediately, put it into a glass jar (filled to the top) and put a lid on it to prevent oxidation. Juice rapidly loses therapeutic and nutritional value during storage.
- Raw fruits and vegetables are not always compatible when eaten together. Apples are the exception. You can also mix pears with Jicama.
- Melons should be juiced by themselves. Making the entire meal melon is an option.
- Avoid using pre-bottled or sweetened juices. All the live enzymes are inactivated when they are pasteurized.
- Juices don't stimulate acids to be released from the stomach, but orange and tomato juice are high in acids and you should mix these juices with other less acidic ones.
- Don't add more than 25% green juice to your vegetable juices. (Unless you have a barf bucket handy!)
- Juicing Greens--you should do this in between harder vegetables, as the juice sludges at the bottom and doesn't pour out easily if you juice them first.

- Dilute all fruit juice with water (one part juice to 2-4 parts water) and drink throughout the day. We've found that 2 cups fruit juice blended with ½ tray of ice cubes comes up to 4 cups--the perfect dilution and it's frothy cold.
- Vegetable juices need not be diluted.

Whole-Day Fasting

This kind of fasting requires you to eat every day but only once. Some people prefer to eat dinner and then nothing else until the following day's dinner. That brings the fasting time to 24 hours, dinner to dinner or lunch to lunch, which is the one I would suggest to you and that definitely worked the best for me. Until you're not completely used to get all of of your calories from one meal (and I'm also talking from a mentality standpoint) it may be difficult for your body to operate optimally. The main challenges you may be facing is around dinner time, our body could get really hungry and that could drive you to consume not-so-great, calorie-dense aliments. Think about it: You're not exactly craving broccoli while you're ravenous. Once again tea, maybe flavored, or coffee can come to aid, but pay attention to not drink too much caffeine, which can have harmful effects on your sleep, and if you're not sleeping, you can find yourself brain-fogged during the day, which will make fasting more difficult.

Here Are the Guidelines

- Hours of Fast - I think the easiest is dinner to dinner so about 6PM-6PM. Why? Well, you are asleep part of the time, therefore your body is resting and you are not thinking about food. It seems to flow well with most peoples' schedules. Anytime is okay though, depending upon your schedule.
- Before the Fast - Eat lightly several hours before the fasting period. Don't stuff yourself with solid and heavy food. Eat healthy and light foods only.
- Drink Juice - Drink lots of juice. I favor non-pasteurized green juice and carrot/beet, but any vegetable combo is great. If it's difficult to find non-pasteurized juice, at least buy organic/natural non-filtered juice. Lemon juice with water (made from squeezing organic lemons) is another great way to help the body cleanse. Again, some people use cranberry juice,

but it needs to be pure juice, no sugar or concentrate. Any juice is good, but organic is best, natural only, and it should be only pure juice and water, with no other ingredients.

- Drink Cleansing Tea - Herbal and Green Teas help the process of cleansing your body. There are several fasting and detox teas, my favorites are made by Yogi Tea and Traditional Medicinals, or you can make your own. Cleansing teas and herbs are available at most natural food stores or online. Herbs are an essential way to help the fasting and cleanse process. Drink a few cups during your fast.

- Drink Water - Water will cleanse and filter out toxins. Drink lots of filtered water, which, of course, includes tea and juice. Pure filtered water is essential for your cleanse and overall health.

- Eliminate Toxins - Urinate and have bowel movements as much as you can. You will urinate frequently as you are drinking liquids. Tea and Raw juice, and in particular vegetable juices, will help you eliminate solid waste and cleanse your colon.

Overnight Fasting

When we come to a 12 hours fasting and a 12 hours' period, we talk about overnight fasting. One of the easiest way to fasting, but simplicity is key to anything done well. For instance, you can choose to avoid feeding after dinner, say 7 pm, and start eating only after 7 am the next morning. At the 12-hour mark, autophagy will still come into play, but with milder cellular advantages.

This is the minimum number of hours advised for fasting, but this approach has the bonus of being quick to execute and requires the lead amount of will power. For the most part, you don't have to miss meals; what you do, if anything, is eliminate a snack at bedtime. However, this approach does not completely harness the benefits of fasting. If you're fasting to lose weight, a narrower fasting window ensures you'll have the full benefits on your weight and general health. Use this just as dipping your toe and entering in the correct mind state of fasting. Use this as a launch pad to take off with one to the other fasting types.

Women-specific Methods of Intermittent Fasting

Evidence suggests that Intermittent Fasting affects the bodies of men and women differently. The bodies of women are much more sensitive to small-calorie changes, especially small negative changes in the intake of calories. Since the bodies of women are made for conceiving and growing babies, women's bodies must be sensitive to any sort of changes that may occur in the internal environment of the body to a larger degree than the bodies of men, in order to ensure that it will produce healthy and strong progeny. For this reason, however, some women may have trouble practicing intermittent fasting according to the above methods. These methods may involve too much restriction for the body of a woman, and she may feel some negative effects such as light-headedness or fatigue. In order to prevent this, there are some adjusted methods of intermittent fasting that will work better for women's bodies. This is not to say that women cannot practice IF or fasting of any sort, but that they must keep this in mind when deciding to try a fasting diet. Women can take a modified approach to fasting so that the internal environment of their bodies remains healthy. Some slightly different patterns of IF may be safer and more beneficial for women. We will look at these below.

Crescendo

This method is quite similar to the Eat-Stop-Eat method that we discussed earlier, except that in this one, the hours have been changed slightly. This fasting regimen involves breaking up the week into days, as well as breaking up the days into hours. In this case, the woman would fast for 14 to 16 hours of the day twice a week and eating normally every other day. These fasting days would not be back to back and would not be more than twice per week.

Alternate Day 5:2

Alternatively, she could fast every other day but only for 12-14 hours, eating normally on the days in between. On the fasting days, she would eat 25% of her normal calorie intake, making it a reduction in calories and not a full-blown fast.

14 and 10

This is a modification of the 16 and 8 method described earlier. In this method, the day would be broken up into segments of hours. The woman would fast for 14 hours, leaving a 10-hour window for feeding. Beginning with this modified version will allow her body to become used to fasting. Eventually, when she is comfortable with it, she can change the hours by one hour per day in order to reach 16 and 8.

By reducing the fasting hours to fourteen or less, women can still experience the benefits that IF can have for weight loss and autophagy induction without putting themselves in any danger. This is not to say that women cannot fast in the same way that men can, but that they must start off slowly and gradually increase their hours of fasting so that they do not shock their bodies. When it comes to health, we must acknowledge the fact that the bodies of men and women are built differently and thus will respond differently to changes.

12 and 12

Women can also benefit from reducing their fasting window even further to 12 hours. This method can be beneficial in the beginning, while your body gets used to the fasting, and you can gradually work your way up from here. In this method, you would normally only eat until three hours before you go to sleep, and then you could begin eating again early enough in the morning to have your first meal be breakfast. For example, if you go to bed at 10 pm, you would only eat until 7 pm. Then you could eat breakfast after 7 am. This is beneficial for people who like to eat breakfast and who do not like to begin their day fasted.

For any person, regardless of sex, the best approach to fasting may vary. When it comes to choosing an approach, being flexible is important. With dieting, the most important factor is consistency. The best diet you can choose will be the one that you can constantly maintain for a long enough period of time that your body can adjust, and changes can begin to occur.

Which One to Choose – OMAD, ADF or ESE?

The answer to this question is not a simple one. All three different types of intermittent fasting have their pros and cons, which we will explore here. However, we do believe that periodic use of the OMAD or ADF protocol could be better for women over 50 years old. As always, consult with your doctor before starting an intermittent fasting program to make sure it is safe for you.

OMAD: In the OMAD protocol, you eat all your daily food within an 8-hour time window during your day (such as 12 pm-8 pm). This type of intermittent fasting was shown to improve insulin sensitivity and blood sugar levels in people with Type 2 diabetes who were eating too many carbs. With the OMAD protocol, fasting blood sugar levels were even lower. However, this means that you may have blood sugar swings and go hypoglycemic during or between meals. You may also have some nutrient deficiencies, so it is not recommended for women over 50 years old. Another downside of OMAD is that you will be eating different foods every day. This can cause boredom and hunger cravings.

ADF: In the ADF protocol (All Day Fasting), you can eat all your daily food (vegan-meal plan) at the same time – although this usually results in losing weight quickly because of higher calorie consumption. Some women experience hormone and metabolic shifts while fasting. It has been shown that women over 50 years old may have more problems with weight loss while on an ADF protocol. This is because the way our bodies work slows down after certain age and we are less metabolically efficient in burning fuel (fat). However, a study found that women who fasted for 24 hours had lower fasting glucose levels than those in the control group. The reason why we think intermittent fasting is better for older women is because it helps you break the pattern of regulating your hunger by eating every 2-3 hours and you will have better energy levels during your fast. Older women should note, however, that if you are elderly and your health is not the best, using ADF may result in the opposite— poor health and low energy levels.

ESE: In this eating schedule a person eats 25-30% of their daily calories one time during the day (such as 8 am-5 pm). You can eat whatever you wish within this 8-hour window. This is the best choice for women over 50 years old. It can help with weight loss and improve energy levels. Also, it reduces food cravings, hunger, and brain fog (those pesky feelings of "brain fog" that often happen in the early morning hours after eating a big meal at night).

So, which one to choose? This depends on your goals as well as how healthy you are. If you are healthy and your goals include weight loss, then ESE is definitely the best choice for women over 50 years. If your goal is to be healthy and avoid gaining weight, OMAD may be a better fit.

CHAPTER 10:

The 4 Rules

Too busy to eat? Do you ever feel your social life, exercise routine, and work schedule often conflict with each other? Are you worried that you might not be able to put the time in for both of these things? Why not try intermittent fasting as your answer to this conundrum?

When you are restricting your daily calories intake, what you eat is much more important! Make sure you are not depriving your organism from vital vitamins, nutrients, fats, and proteins it requires to sustain a healthy immune system, recover from injury or disease, keep muscles solid, and keep the metabolism working smoothly. I believe what we eat can deeply influence our life and our health. I decided to include some diet secrets I have been following since day one, as well as realistic fasting schedules and recipes to assist you.

Rule 1: Only Eat Real Food

This means no counterfeit food and no diet-drinks. Chances are you have fond memories of neon orange corn chips, fizzy drinks and sugar packed candies. Hopefully, things have changed and you're enjoying big bowls of rocket and Parmesan salads, roasted artichoke and monkfish. However, the majority of people follow a diet rich in refined, low-fiber, and nutrient-deficient foods. Keep in mind that not all processed food is evil. Food without added sugar or salt and freshly-frozen fruit and vegetables are still a good alternative.

Pay attention to labels that shouts "fat 0%" because that fat is simply substituted with refined sugars (apart from dairy products, where low fat is fine). Most sources of sugar, such as sucrose, maltose, glucose, fructose are all bad for your diet and for your health.

Highly processed foods may also have high levels of chemicals which can have a blocking effect on hormones that regulate weight loss. My advice? When in doubt, keep the meals genuine!

What Makes Up a Real Food Diet?

- **Protein**

Amino acids, also known as the "building blocks of life," are what makes up proteins. They are also vital for the synthesis of hormones and neurotransmitters. We know there are approximately 500 amino acids present in nature, only 20 of them are crucial for our body. These can be divided into essential amino acids and non-essential amino acids. Animal protein such as meat, dairy, fish, and egg contain all the amino acids required.

- **Carbohydrates**

In diet and weight loss, carbs are one of the most contentious subjects. We have been advised for years that we can eat so much fat and that the primary source of heart disease is saturated fat. However, some scientists have recently disputed this assumption, arguing that carbs are especially to blame for the obesity crisis and a slew of other diseases.

The body searches for calories in its glycogen reserves while it is starved of carbohydrates. Fats (the good ones) and healthy carbs are needed. It's useless and potentially risky to completely avoid carbohydrates. Not all carbohydrates are in fact equal. Carbohydrates with a low caemic index (GI) found in fiber-rich fruits, beans, unrefined grains and vegetables are important to maintain a healthy organism and can, for example, actively promote weight loss by decreasing appetite. On the other hand, High-GI processed carbs, such as those found in soft drinks, white bread, pastries, some breakfast cereals and sweeteners, have to be avoided since they can affect long-term health. Studies proved the risk of heart failure and Type 2 diabetes rises when eating a lot of high-GI carbohydrates.

- **Fat**

Since fat is the most caloric nutrient, regulating and controlling your fat consumption will help you in your battle for weight loss. Fat, however, plays a crucial part in every diet because it contains the essential acids required for the absorption of vitamins. A lack of fats in your diet can contribute to a number of health issues. If you consume the right kinds of fat in the right quantities, fats will make you feel full longer. That's why I don't want you to think of fat as your enemy, but more as a supporting friend in your search for a healthy lifestyle! Adding a little of the right fat to your meals assists in nutrient absorption and, some would say, increases the taste of your food. Monounsaturated fats or oils (such as olive oil and rapeseed oil) are safer for your heart. As it is heat-stable, coconut oil can be a decent option for cooking too.

- **Fruit**

Some people say that fruits can make you gain weight. They guarantee weight gain can be caused even by a modest intake. Most people with a clear understanding of nutrition, however, are conscious that this is not entirely true. As always, balance is key. Carbohydrates (10-20%), water, fibres, vitamins, enzymes, minerals, and other nutrients are all contained in berries. Carbs are the only element that adds to nutrition. Since most fruits produce only around 10 percent, to get 3 1/2 oz (100 g) of carbs, you will need to consume 2.2 lb (1 kg) of apples. You will only need about 7 oz (a few hundred grammes) and about 10 oz (300 g) of pasta or bread to get the same amount of carbs. Since more than that is used by the brain only (an average of 4 1/2 oz [120-130 g] of carbohydrates every day), eating a significant quantity of fruit per day is not an issue.

- **Whole Grain**

We may count whole grain bread, whole wheat noodles, whole grain cereals and brown rice among the variety of whole grain products, as well as flax seeds, quinoa, oatmeal, barley and rye. For all these products, the common denominator is that the seed/grain preserves the bran (the "shell") and includes fibre, vitamin B, and trace elements. Moreover, the part known as germ, is rich in vitamins and antioxidants. Refined foods preserve only the endosperm, which includes only starch, protein, and a slight amount of fat, as well as fragments of fibre, vitamins, minerals, and antioxidants. Whole grain alternatives should be favoured over processed grain alternatives for genuinely healthy food. There's one downside to big quantities of whole grain, though: sensitive stomachs can suffer, so a balance has to be found to not overdo your whole grain intake. Consuming whole grains is healthy both for your wellbeing and for your weight. They are digested more slowly than refined one, keeping the levels of insulin and sugar down.

Rule 2: Skip the Sugar

Sugar makes you obese and encourages your skin to age prematurely. Sugar is associated with collagen and elastin and decreases skin elasticity, making you look older than your age. To add a little flavour, the recipes you may cook should use low-sugar fruits and the occasional drizzle of a natural sweetener such as honey, which is perfect and tastes amazing. Sugar is usually harmful for you and you must quit it.

If you need a sweet fix, stick to dark chocolate. You will need less that your normal super processed sweet to feel satisfied and happy.

Rule 3: Watch the Alcohol

The alcohol level in most alcoholic beverages has risen over time. Remember that a drink will have more alcohol than you may think. Two units may be contained in a tiny glass of wine (175ml/5½fl oz/ cup). Alcohol, besides not being the best companion of life, brings with it useless calories. If you're looking to lose weight, consider cutting it down, or better yet, don't drink any. For a woman the a limit is two units of alcohol per day; for a male, three units can suffice. A single pub measure (25ml/3⁄4fl oz) of alcohol, for example, is around one unit, and one or one and a half units is half a pint of lager, wine, bitter or beer.

If you can't miss the thrill of holding the glass in your hand, you'd better enjoy a soft drink or an alcohol-free grape juice as a delightful wine alternative. Alcohol-free drinks are becoming more and more popular.

Rule 4: Eat Fruit, Don't Drink It

If you drink 1 litre (35fl oz/4 cups) of fruit juice, bear in mind that you'll be eating 500 calories. That's good if you're fasting with juice, but too much if it's just a snack. For the same number of calories, you might eat a baked potato with tuna and two slices of fruit.

Pick herbal teas (especially green tea, which may aid fat loss) instead. You are welcome to have a cup of tea or coffee. Usually, in most intermittent fasting plan, tiny quantities of milk are allowed, but hold it to a splash.

When fasting, drink lots of water; try to go for a fluid consumption of 1.22 litres (4070fl oz/ 8 cups) each day. Not only can this serve to keep hunger pangs at bay, but it will keep you hydrated as well.

Rule 5: Avoid the Pitfalls

1. When you begin fasting, you may feel hungry at those times when you would usually feed, especially if you used to eat sugary snacks. You may feel light-headed, but this is not an indication you are wasting away or entering starvation mode, because after the regular meal time has passed, these thoughts of hunger will usually subside. Try to get your source of carbs from fruits, veggies, and whole grains. Consume a decent portion of protein that fills you up for longer. This is really simple once you get used to eat healthy and understand your body.

2. For quick meals, stock up. Make sure you still have recipes on hand for quick-to-prepare meals like stir-fries, soups, and salads in your refrigerator and cupboards.

3. If you have kids or grandkids, don't polish their plates off. Eating leftovers from children is a fast way for parents and grandparents to add weight. When the kids are done with their dinner, place the dishes directly into the sink or dishwasher, so you would not be tempted!

4. Minimize the size of the dinner plate. A great deal of our appetite and pleasure are psychological. We can feel scarcity of food as we see a large plate only half full. However, we can easily fool our mind if the plate is tiny but appears full with the same amount of food; we subconsciously think we have consumed enough.

5. Don't be fooled by the typical "frappucoffee" mixture of milkshake and coffee typical of the most famous fhranchises. That is not equivalent of coffee. Black coffee only contains about 10 calories, but for a regular small cappuccino, a milky coffee can contain anywhere from 100 calories to a whopping

350+ calories for a grand with all the toppings. In the same fashion you shortened your plate size, shrink your cup size and the waistlinewill follow. Don't think about asking for half the milk. Do your own coffee and don't fill the cup to the brim. Less is more when it comes to the joy of savoring the little things.

6. Sandwich is the go-to carb-heavy snack. If you must eat it for time constraints cut the processed carbs losing the top slice of bread and load it up with green salad leaves and few balanced dressing instead.

7. You don't have to make all these life changes at once. You can take it slow, nobody is chasing you, only you. You decide the pace, because you are your best person to assess how your body is doing. Focus on one step at a time.

8. Make sure the portions are right. If you're reducing the number of meals you consume, it stands to reason the portion sizes should be higher than if you were eating more mini-meals a day. Use the recipe section as a guide to decide the size of your portions.

9. If you're a mom, or you have baby grandchildren, pick carefully the meals you want to skip. I've attempted fasting with a toddler who couldn't understand why mummy was not eating and one day decided to shove a fistful of tuna pasta into my mouth. Be mindful of the example that you're giving.

Rule 6: Go Easy on the Bacon

Let's speak about the saturated fats known as LCT, or long-chained fats, which are plentiful in fatty animal products like sausages, pork, fatty beef, and lard. Dairy fats produce around 35% LCT too, however they often contain many other fats that mitigate LCT's harmful impact. Physiologically, LCTs are the best fats in terms of being processed for further use by the liver. They are fat-soluble and, as a result, can survive in fat cells (unlike SCT and MCT); additionally, they do not go rancid. This suggests that LCTs can be retained for longer periods, a trick human bodies have acquired during evolution, and there are a variety of pathways that influence weight gain by making long-chained saturated fats. First and foremost, LCTs decrease insulin sensitivity, which means that more insulin is needed to maintain blood sugar regulation (to unlock the cells, so that blood sugar is absorbed). Insulin is also a hormone that helps the digestion of fats by fat cells. As a result, more insulin makes us fatter!

Since it takes time for insulin sensitivity to deteriorate, a mixture of fats at each meal can have a detrimental effect. Higher insulin and blood sugar levels are caused by eating habits with a large presence of saturated fats, compared to diary regimen with more unsaturated fats. As the saturated fat intake increases, fat burning tends to decline. Today we have far too many overweight children with excessive belly fat whose diets rely on daily high doses of saturated fats rather than watching closely what they eat. I find this terrifying.

The Wrong Saturated Fats Are Difficult to Digest

Long-chained saturated fats seem to be slower to metabolise than monounsaturated or polyunsaturated fats throughout the muscles. Olive oil, avocado, rapeseed oil, and fish are rich in monounsaturated and polyunsaturated fats. Long-chained saturated fats are more difficult for the body to burn during exercise, according to reports. This is important for both those who want to lose weight and those who want to improve their stamina and general health to slow down aging.

Products to Avoid if You Want to Burn Fat:

- Bacon
- Pork belly
- Fatty sausages
- Minced pork
- Tallow
- Too many fatty dairy products (cream, butter, cheese)

Foods to Avoid
Canola Oil

Interestingly, it contains hemagglutinins. A component which is also present in mustard gas! This explains why it is being associated with respiratory illnesses. Furthermore, canola oil acts as an acetyl chlonisterase inhibitor which disrupts the nerve and muscle signal transmission. This can lead to multiple sclerosis (MS).

Like how other oils are being extracted, hexane is also being used. An industrial chemical that is a waste product of gasoline! This makes canola loaded with unhealthy trans-fatty acids. A study where rats, were used as subjects, clearly shows that canola launched their unhealthy trans-fatty acids so high in their system.

Many alternatives can be used other than this controversial oil. To avoid pesticide oil, use olive oil. According to the World Journal of Gastroenterology (2009), olive oil, along with the Mediterranean diet, is an excellent food for healthy heart, liver, and blood sugar regulation. Don't forget coconut oil too! In its purest form, it contains 50% lauric acid. It is the substance that fastens coconut oil as one of the healthiest super foods. Coconut oil has anti-fungal and anti-bacterial properties. It can cure so many conditions: from athlete's foot, influenza, hepatitis C and many more. It just simply boosts your immune system!

Energy Bars

In this fast-paced world, it is common to see someone grab an energy bar and eat it on their way to their office or whatever duties one needs to attend to. Although commercial energy bars give you an instant boost of liveliness, the duration of the rush wears down almost instantly as well. What's worst, it will leave you hungrier than before. Don't be deceived by the misleading tags such as "complete" and "healthy" along with its flashy advertisements because energy bars are definitely one of the foods you need to avoid for healthier living.

The most popular energy bars' main protein source is soy protein. The process undergoes for consumption is disturbing. Hexane, an industrial by-product of gasoline, is mixed with soy beans to extract its oil. It is used by other industries for purposes like clearing printing machines of its greasiness and also as a solvent for glues and inks. According to the Environmental Protection Agency (EPA), it is an air pollutant. But especially to humans, the solvent is a strong chemical that poses dangers to neurological health.

Casein, a protein derived from cow's milk, can also be found in most bars. There are three types of casein: native whole milk, cheese, and industrial. And what's included in popular energy bars? You guessed it right –industrial! Such chemical is linked to tumor growth in the colon and cancer.

Though many energy bars are dangerous to health, there is still a lot that comes from organic sources. Even if you are in a rush, don't forget to take time to scan the ingredients. Now, you know what ingredients are to be avoided. If there is a non-genetically modified fruit stand on your way, why not stop for those instead?

Margarine

Margarine and butter are both fats. Both are controversial, but the latter is definitely better. What makes margarine dangerous to one's well-being is its hydrogenation process. It is done to prolong its shelf life and to maintain its solid form at room temperature. This is another example of commercial convenience made greater when the health value of a food should be a priority. The end result of this process turns its fats from saturated to unsaturated form.

This kind of fat is the type that buildups and obstructs the arteries and veins of an individual and ultimately results in heart attack, stroke and other deadly diseases. A study in Harvard even declared that margarine could be to blame for the 30,000 yearly deaths from cardiovascular diseases. A publication released by the American Journal of Public Health stated that the fats found in margarine are worst than the fats found in butter and meats.

In addition, because margarine is based on vegetable oils, the common preservative used is butylated hydroxytoluene (BHT), which is an additive linked to neurological damage and cancer.

The good news is you don't need to stick to the unhealthy substitute but rather resort to the original —butter. However, be careful about your consumption of butter as everything in excess is harmful to health. Butter, without the unnecessary additives, is packed with vitamins and trace minerals. It contains vitamin A, selenium, zinc and magnesium. Conjugated linoic acid (CLA) which is beneficial to the respiratory system especially to asthmatics is also present. Butter is great for the prevention of arthritis as well since wulzen factor is one of its nutritional components.

Microwaveable Popcorn

In fact, what gives the microwaveable popcorn its taste and aroma is far from butter. The chemical responsible is called Diacetyl (DA). The artificial flavoring that is directly linked to irreversible respiratory sickness called bronchiolitis obliterans. It is the partial or complete obstruction of the small airways in the lungs (called bronchioles) as a result of inflammation and the formation of scar tissues in the area.

Bronchiolitis obliterans was so much linked to the artificial popcorn flavoring that the disease is also referred to as "popcorn lung." The name was attributed because several popcorn factory workers that use diacetyl have contracted respiratory disease.

Canned Foods

National Health and Nutrition Examination Survey (NHANES) of the US revealed in 2010 how much of the population are exposed to the fatal chemical bisphenol-A. 95% of the partakers in the survey showed high amounts of BPA in them. Why we all are exposed to it? Because BPA is found in plastics and almost all canned goods!

Bisphenol-A is a resin added to the linings of a can to prevent its contents to have a metallic taste. It also prolongs its shelf life as it barricades the metal from the food to prevent it from spoiling fast.

BPA is associated with coronary heart disease and many other detrimental illnesses. It disrupts the function of the endocrine system as it imitates the effects of the hormone estrogen. This eventually results in mood changes, abnormalities in metabolism, and a decline in sexual and reproductive ability.

Soda

Regular drinkers of pop know by experience how hard it is to get rid of the habit. Caffeine is the answer to why. Coffee beans naturally have caffeine; but why add it in soda pop? It was claimed that it adds a distinct flavor to it. But a blind study of John Hopkins Medical Institution revealed that only 8% can identify what is with caffeine or not.

The intake of caffeine leads to chemical dependence. Thus, it makes them irritable after a couple of hours of withdrawal. They end up drinking time and again: a slow and deadly cycle that leads to many conditions (from insomnia to heart attack).

That's just one reason why sodas made it on the list; another is because of its artificial sweetener. Almost all of the soda pop, you can find are sweetened by High Fructose Corn Syrup (HFCS). This maybe the sweetest poison there is that the modern population is heavily ingesting. According to the journal Environmental Health, HFCS contains mercury. This liquid silver is a potent neurotoxin!

Further studies tied soda pop to why it should be avoided if you want to live longer. According to a publication from the Institute of Medicine (2012), soda pop is a "major contributor of obesity." A British medical journal, The Lancet, also came up with the same conclusion stating that 12-year-old who are drinkers of soda are most likely to become obese.

Processed Meats

Do you enjoy eating bacon, hotdogs, sausages, and hams? It is time to stop eating those meats according to an internationally recognized body when it comes to cancer. That is what they found out after 7000 studies. In 2007, after a colossal series of studies for 5 years, it was announced by World Cancer Research Fund (WCRF) that "no amount of processed meat" can be considered harmless. If you want to live a long sound life, it is time to end the consumption of these lethal meats.

Do you wonder why processed meats are so brightly red? When meats are fresh, its color is red—only for a short while. On the other hand, processed meats stay red for a very long time because of the additive sodium nitrate. However, it does not give any nutritional value to the meat but rather makes it very cancerous: from the pancreas, breast, prostate, gut, to the brain.

Another additive that makes processed meats certainly unhealthy is monosodium glutamate. MSG makes foods so tasty but at the same time so toxic. MSG is a neurotoxin that causes Alzheimer's disease, dementia, and migraine.

Low Fat

The most effective way to stay healthy and prevent blood vessels from being clogged with cholesterol is to eat products tagged "low fat." Except that it is false. Most health-conscious consumers are easily deceived by advertisements of this kind of claim. The fact is fats are vital to the overall health of an individual. Yes, there are bad fats but there are goods fats as well. And "low fat" products are not the ones that you are looking for. Don't cut out fats but balance it with protein and carbohydrates.

New England Journal of Medicine (2008) had studied which eating habits, such as low fat and the Mediterranean diet, can do for optimal health. According to the findings, a low-fat diet had an insignificant effect on weight and worsened cholesterol, while a low carbohydrate diet was found the most beneficial.

A low-fat diet will only tend you to carbohydrate packing, which raises the level of insulin in the blood. This will result in high blood sugar. The excess sugar in the blood will be turning the surplus of energy into cholesterol and fats.

Sugar-Free

You are a sweet tooth strolling the market for a snack, you see a product written "sugar-free!" on its label. You cashed it in and enjoyed it at home guilt-free. The bad news, sugar-free products may have done more harm to you than goods that actually contain sugar. Although limiting the intake of sugar is good for the health, eating foods containing the alternative sweetener aspartame is very much unhealthy and should be avoided.

Discovered in 1965, aspartame or acesulfame potassium was deemed dangerous after several studies. Up to date, its distribution and legalities stay controversial. It was found out that aspartame is actually cancerous. It is made up of asparctic acid, phenylalanine, and methanol.

Asparctic acid was declared greatly damaging to the brain by Dr. John Olney of his study in Washington School of Medicine. The findings state that the animals subjected to the acid developed holes in their brain. While phenylalanine plays it part as a mood killer and leaves an individual in depression.

Methanol turns into formaldehyde once metabolized in the body, which leads to cancer! Other harmful effects of methanol are headaches, diarrhea, dementia, brain tumors, diabetes and many more. Formaldehyde is in fact used as finishers of textiles, a very strong disinfectant and an embalming agent!

Most aspartame-containing products are foods labeled "sugar-free," diet sodas, flavored water, and chewing gums. While staying away from those products, you can use stevia as a safe and healthy substitute. Stevia had been known to lower blood pressure and blood sugar, making it perfect for the prevention of heart diseases and diabetes. It is definitely one of the best natural sweeteners you could substitute for sugar.

Fast Foods

There's no other best way to conclude this section except for serving facts about popular fast-food chains. Their menus are a list of foods that should be avoided because of the many hidden dangers that come with it. It's like a summary of what you've read here plus other additional toxic substances you've never heard of!

Starting from the source of their beef, it might be right when you think it's from an old farmer that had a farm, but kids will not sing to their advertising anthems once they knew what processes are done in that place. Most popular chains keep their animals: in a nasty sanitary condition, they're injected with antibiotics, and are genetically modified.

According to the journal Annals of Diagnostic Pathology, the real meat in most of the burger patties in eight of the most popular food chains are actually only 2%! Mostly water; other fillers are composed of animals' arteries and veins, nerves, body fats, and bones.

Natural salt is 40% sodium, but for flavor enhancing purposes, most popular fast foods use unnatural salt which has so much elevated sodium in it. Regular ingestion of this inevitably gives you hypertension. Excessive sugar and high fructose corn syrup is used to improve sweetness. Excessive sugar intake ultimately leads to diabetes and other dangerous diseases while HFCS is found out to contain mercury. Monosodium glutamate (MSG) is also a common ingredient that has been giving fast food lovers their migraines, diarrhea and many other conditions. Dimethylpolysiloxane, an anti-foaming agent and a sealant, is present as well.

As always, convenience should not be valued above the nutritional value you are eating. As much as possible, avoid fast foods and make sure it's natural. Take time to read what's on the label and the ingredients of what you buy from groceries. Be aware of the packages that could be toxic to health. It's important to have a balanced diet and daily exercise. Enjoy Life and live it wise, long, and vigorous!

Essential Oils: The Power of Perfumes

When you look at the essential oils from their medicinal properties, they can help with everything, from elevating our mood, to helping your body heal, and beyond. Smelling certain essential blends will reduce your appetite. The following list of essential oils will have their Latin names included because one common name can refer to two or three different essential oils.

Bergamot (Citrus bergamia)

This citrus essential oil strengthens your emotions and helps with depression and stress. This is often good to use during weight loss because your emotional state needs to be in a good place to help you lose weight and keep it off. The only warning to be careful of is going out in the sun directly after a blend with bergamot in it. It can cause sensitivity to the sun.

Carrot Seed (Daucus carota)

This essential oil is used in cases of sensitive skin and can help with water retention. Best avoided during pregnancy and breastfeeding.

Cedarwood, Virginia (Juniperus virginiana)

This oil is good for helping prevent water retention and is also good for smoothing cellulite. Can cause skin irritation.

Cinnamon (Cinnamomum zeylanicum)

This is the leaf of the tree. The bark is too volatile to use. It helps maintain your energy levels, which comes in handy before or during workouts or for a long day at work. It helps to combat fatigue. Avoid if you are taking blood thinners, are pregnant or breast feeding, or have overly sensitive skin.

Coriander Seed (Coriandrum sativum)

This essential oil is good for all types of digestive problems and disorders. It helps to detoxify cells and aids in fighting mental fatigue.

Cypress (Cupressus sempervirens)

This helps with circulation issues which can hamper exercise and helping to prevent the retention of fluid. Avoid using this one too often, and avoid altogether if you are pregnant or breastfeeding.

Eucalyptus Peppermint (Eucalyptus dives)

There are four different kinds of Eucalyptus. This one can help the body smooth out bumps due to cellulite. It also helps fight fatigue and exhaustion. Please, avoid this essential oil if you are pregnant.

Fennel (Foeniculum vulgare)

This essential oil comes in handy when you want to smooth cellulite or help your body correct water retention. It also helps with digestive issues which can prevent your body from absorbing nutrients.

Don't use if you are taking a lot of prescription medications. Avoid if pregnant or breastfeeding.

Frankincense (Boswellia carteri)

Since stubborn fat tends to hang around because of stress, this essential oil helps in that regard. It also helps with mental fatigue.

Ginger (Zingiber officinale)

This is an immune booster that can also stimulate the body as a whole. Ginger is also good to add to blends as a catalyst.

Grapefruit (Citrus paradisi)

This essential oil is recommended when you're trying to lose weight, smooth out cellulite, purge any retained fluids, and it even helps to keep your spirits up. Try not to use it if you are taking multiple prescription medications.

Greenland Moss (Ledum groenlandicum)

This little known essential oil helps to promote a healthy liver, helps to boost the body during weight loss, and helps to prevent water retention.

Jasmine (Jasminum grandiforum)

This oil is used in weight loss blends to help with stress, feelings of low self-esteem, and fatigue.

Lemon (Citrus limon)

This oil helps with digestive problems. It helps to detox cells, and also helps the body to get rid of cellulite.

Lemongrass (Cymbopogon flexuosus)

This detoxifying essential oil can also help smooth cellulite and as well helps with exhaustion.

Lime (Citrus auranifolia)

Helps with loss of appetite, detoxifies, and helps to smooth cellulite.

Mandarin (Citrus reticulata)

This helps with cellulite and digestive disorders.

Orange (Citrus sinesis)

This helps with the retention of fluid, smooths cellulite, and helps to raise spirits and stress.

Peppermint (Mentha piperita)

It helps with all sorts of digestive problems that can prevent proper weight loss. It can also help with fatigue. Avoid in the early stages of pregnancy.

Rosemary (Rosmarius officinalis)

This essential oil is recommended for smoothing cellulite, improving circulation. It also helps to detoxify cells, too. Avoid if pregnant.

Saro (Cinnamosma fragrans)

This is another little known essential oil on the mass market, but it comes in handy when smoothing cellulite.

Violet Leaf (Viola odora)

This helps with water retention, cellulite, and helps to tone the skin.

CHAPTER 11:

Prolonged Fasting

D o you know what a prolonged fast is? A prolonged fast can last anywhere from 1 to 7 or more days. At the end of the time, a person is not allowed any food or drink anything besides water and tea. This will discuss the benefits of this type of fasting and how it could change your life for the better. Here are some facts about prolonged fasting:

- It allows your organs to rest and do less work than usual.
- It boosts your body's regenerative capacity by triggering autophagy, which facilitates healing.
- It improves immune system function; in other words, it makes you healthier (especially as you get older).
- It reduces the presence of stress hormones in the body and reduces inflammation.
- It boosts your energy level, making it easier for you to get through long fasts.
- Longer fasts actually make people feel less hungry.
- You become more aware of your senses and can feel what your body is saying to you.
- While you're doing long fasts, you'll become more able to control emotions like anger, fear, anxiety and sadness.
- You'll also become better at listening to your breath or heartbeat as part of daily practice.

"Prolonged fasting is when someone abstains from eating food for a period of time longer than 24 hours. This could be a full week, 48 hours or more. It has been used since ancient times as a tool for healing, helping people recover from disease and generally improving their quality of life. It can also be used to deepen spiritual practice and awareness."

Here are some benefits of prolonged fasting:

1. Clearer thinking:

Prolonged fasts reduce the levels of stress hormones in your body, which clears your mind and makes it easier for you to access higher levels of consciousness. You'll notice you think more clearly about your problems and solutions. Your mood will be improved as well, because as the other hormones in your body are balanced out, you'll feel less sad or angry.

2. Improved metabolism:

Fasting actually works to reduce the formation of fat in your body, and also makes it easier for you to burn off the fat that's already been made. This means prolonged fasting could help you lose weight!

3. A better immune system:

Prolonged fasting can improve your resistance to disease in many ways, but the main one is that it triggers autophagy inside your cells. Autophagy is a self-cleaning process that clears out junk and damaged cellular structures within the cells themselves–this includes pathogens, damaged proteins and even damaged organelles inside mitochondria. The body's ability to clear these types of debris is necessary for the immune system to function well. Autophagy is also necessary for the repair of damaged nerve tissue and the formation of new neurons (as your brain cells are constantly being destroyed and replaced).

4. Improved sleep:

Your sleep quality will improve when you're fasting as well, because you'll have an easier time controlling your nerves and hormones. With a better sleep schedule, you'll naturally have better memory during the day, and less anxiety–and this will definitely make you happier!

5. Better focus:

When you've fasted for 48 hours, your brain cells will begin to slow down, allowing you to focus better on your objectives. You might even be able to achieve a level of enlightenment without actually meditating!

6. Less fuel consumption:

You won't be eating during your fast (other than water and tea), so your body will naturally consume less fuel (calories). Since you'll be burning more calories through exercise and meditation, this could actually help you lose weight.

7. A deeper connection with your spiritual side:

If you're doing a prolonged fast as part of your spiritual practice, you should expect to make progress at a faster rate. You'll have access to higher levels of consciousness and vibrate on a higher plane during this time. You may also discover there's more than one universe.

8. More energy:

One of the biggest benefits of prolonged fasting is increased energy levels, which may seem contradictory at first. This is because when you start fasting, the nutrients in your body are concentrated inside certain organs like the brain and liver (which need them to function properly). As a result, your body uses less fuel to run itself and you have more energy. You'll actually feel less hungry during your fast, because your body will be getting most of what it needs from your organs.

9. Loss of excess weight:

The prolonged fast will clean out your cells, which will reduce the amount of fat that's built up in the body. This is especially useful for people who are a little overweight but don't want to use crash diets (which can be dangerous).

10. Improved brain function:

If you're doing a 24-day fast, your brain will be the strongest it will ever be. [Fasting blood-spans in stroke victims are typically 18% to 30% longer when they fast for 2 weeks.] Prolonged fasting also helps get rid of the free radicals that can damage brain cells.

11. More mental clarity:

Prolonged fasts should make you more aware of your state of mind and what you're thinking about during your meditation. This should lead to faster progress when doing any type of spiritual work, like meditation or visualization exercises.

12. Increased blood oxygenation:

Dr. Seyfried, a neuro-oncologist who has spent years studying cancer and the brain, showed in his book Cancer as a Metabolic Disease that prolonged fasts cause numerous improvements in the body's ability to deliver and utilize oxygen. This helps reduce your risk of stroke, since chewing food actually increases your risk of blood clots (due to the increase in platelets caused by chewing). This also means you'll have a higher resistance to fatigue.

13. Improved tissue and organ function:

During your fast, your body will be able to devote more energy towards repairing and improving the functioning of your organs. The brain is one of the most important organs, so it gets the most attention during a fast. You may have noticed you have more mental clarity after a prolonged fast (especially if you're doing one as part of your spiritual practice). This is because it allows you to access more information about yourself and others.

14. Increased longevity:

As all 10 points above show, there are numerous ways in which prolonged fasting can dramatically improve your body's ability to fight off disease symptoms like fatigue, aches and pains, brain fog or depression (and that's just naming a few). People who fast regularly have significantly lower rates of the following chronic diseases:

a) Stroke
b) Diabetes, Type 2
c) Cancer, especially brain tumors
d) Alzheimer's and Parkinson's disease
e) Coronary heart disease, also called a heart attack, is a condition in which the blood flow to the heart is insufficient (caused by atherosclerosis). If you see any of the warning signs — such as chest pain or shortness of breath (especially when you're exercising) — you should go to the hospital right away and ask for a death certificate [unless you want your family members to go through a lot of hassle].

f) Retinopathy (eye disease). This is a condition where the retina of your eye suffers from bleeding or detached from your eyewall.

g) Intestinal blockage, or Crohn's disease

Moreover, it is always imperative to consume vegan supplements from plant based sources of nutrients and vitamins your diet may be devoid of, such as Vitamin B12, Nascent Iodine, and Vitamin D3, to ensure your body has all the required nutrients it needs to attain robust, vigorous health. By eating only fruits and vegetables that have low glycemic loads and are characterized by high levels of alkalinity, meaning they leave an alkaline residue of 7.0 or above post being digested, you can attain an alkaline body and perhaps even circumvent the formation of tumors since cancer cells need an acidic environment to survive, prosper, and proliferate. The only part of the vessel that should be highly acidic is the stomach, with a PH level of 6 or below, to disintegrate anything that enters into it. In that way, your organism does not become a repository for waste and store food products for prolonged periods of time in the form of belly fat.

It is always incumbent to get your blood tested to ensure your body has all the nutrients it needs for optimal health at all times. You can refine your diet as need by incorporating a wider variety of nutrient dense fruits and vegetables into your diet if your blood tests indicate your body is lacking a nutrient, such as non-heme iron. By having access to the blood test results, you can make dietary changes, such as by profusely eating olives in this example to rectify an iron deficiency you might be succumbing to encountering.

Before you undergo a prolonged fast, you want to ensure that you have a healthy BMI of well above 18.5, have recently consumed a copious amount of nutrient dense fruits and vegetables to nourish the vessel, are eminently hydrated, and do not have to do anything too physical intense amid this fasting period. I personally attempt to eat 5,000-20,000 calories per meal before undergoing a prolonged fast.

Amid the prolonged fasting time, you can enter ketosis within a 24-hour period by dry fasting or alternatively enter ketosis within a 72-hour period by water fasting. If you opt to dry fast only for the initial 24 hours, you can enter ketosis in one-third the time then you otherwise would if you were going to water fast through the entirety of the prolonged fast. It is always advised to be eminently hydrated and never dehydrated. Furthermore, if you opt to dry fast for the initial 24 hours amid the prolonged fast then you should always drink distilled water after the 24-hour period has elapsed. I personally do not go for any longer than 24 hours without distilled water.

A prolonged fast is typically 24-96 hours in length and can be utilized as the panacea combined with a raw fruitarian diet to help you optimize health, maximize your longevity rate, and avert succumbing to chronic diseases.

As frugivores with long intestines, high PH levels, and flat teeth, it is incumbent that our species only devours foods from foods groups that we have the anatomy to efficaciously digest, such as fruits and vegetables. It is unwise to devour animal carcasses, animal secretions, synthetic products, oils, refined grains, whole grains, and oxidized products if the individual is looking to optimize their health, minimize inflammation, prolong their life, and mitigate as many health risks as possible. We currently cannot modify our innate genetic code and should ideally resort to following a diet of only consuming fruits and vegetables that optimize our health and maximize our longevity rate.

Fruits and vegetables are chalk full of vitamins, minerals, carotenoids, phytonutrients, antioxidants, fiber, and other salubrious compounds that we need to be able to thrive, prosper, and flourish. The health benefits reaped and the nutrient profiles will vary per fruit or vegetable, with some foods being far healthier to consume than others.

Extended Water Fasting

You can go for a long time without food but not water. The longer you go without food, the more weight you will lose, the longer you will remain in ketosis, and the more time you give your body to heal and repair. If you set a time frame to drink only water and nothing else for several days in a row, you are doing an extended water fast. You can add a little sea salt to your water for electrolytes, but do not introduce anything else to make your metabolism run. Of course, it is a simple process but hard to implement. It is not for the "faint of heart," as they say. You need to prepare yourself mentally for this challenge. Your body will send all sorts of signals during this process to get you to eat something. It is a mental game more than a physical one for most people. Before starting this fast, you need to be aware of the challenges you will face from fatigue, irritability, hunger "pains," and brain fog. These are all the side effects of your body changing from glucose to fat or insulin reliance to ketosis. But then, you also have the neuropathways that have been developed over many years of eating that release ghrelin at set times according to your circadian rhythms. This is the hunger chemical that tells your body it is time to eat, even if you are not really hungry. It seems like real hunger, but it is really just a programmed response. You need to break this habit in your body, but it takes time to get over it.

Fasting in History:

Fasting is practiced as a means of religious devotion or spiritual discipline. In some religions, it is also done as a form of penance. Fasting is most often seen in the context of Christian fasting, which lasts from Wednesday evening until Saturday evening inclusive. It is also practiced in other branches of Judaism and Islam, among other faiths. The word fasting comes from the Latin fasto, which means "temporary abstention from food or drink." The Interreligious Foundation for Fasting and Prayer promotes communal fasting during Lent in the United States.

In religion, a fast is an act of abstinence or discipline, intended to prepare the soul and body for a period of self-denial and penance (similar to confession). While many practices involve abstinence from one or more foods ("fasting"), this is not always the case. Many programs that promote physical exercise also promote abstinence from food during exercise. Fasting is undertaken for a variety of spiritual reasons. Some believe fasting helps develop spirituality and purity.

A person who practices intermittent fasting will occasionally eat for a period of time but will follow this with two or more days without food or caloric beverages (such as water). In general, fasting involves giving up food and drink for an extended period because one believes that it helps to focus one's thoughts on God (for example by bringing them closer to God) or to gain spiritual enlightenment. Fasting as a religious exercise is believed to have originated in pre-Christian Europe. The practice was brought to America by early European immigrants. In the 20th century. The spread of fasting as an international custom was due in part to Harvey Kellogg's work. Kellogg, a surgeon, created Corn Flakes and established the Sanitas Food Company to promote health and good nutrition. Kellogg believed that fasting, especially when accompanied by prayer and bible study, could promote spiritual well-being. Fasting may also be practiced out of mourning or self-discipline.

Do you know how the word "breakfast" came about?

We know that breakfast is the first meal you take after a night's sleep. However, the term is revealing as it means breaking a fast of the night before, which you did when you slept. From the term, you get a glimpse of fasting as a natural biological tendency of man to give the body rest, balance, and save energy after a day's work or during critical times. For instance, you lose your appetite in times of stress or when you feel sick. Fasting is a natural healing therapy used by the early people, which continued to the present.

Fasting in Primitive People

Fasting has older roots in primitive times, with dietary restrictions referred to by the primitive people as 'taboo.' Considered taboos are certain vegetables and animals, and eating of specific food during particular days of the year. These people practice dietary restrictions for health and safety reasons. However, artifacts exist that depict not only restrictions but fasting or abstinence from food.

Fasting for the primitive people was motivated by:

Special rituals. Primitive people fasts during important events, like initiating their youth into adulthood. Fasting could last from 24 hours to days. They also fast before the consumption of a new harvest, before engaging in a tribal war, and before hunting. Purification. Purification of the body is similar to the modern-day concept; the difference lies in the purpose. For primitive people, purifying the body is to prepare it for a purpose, to give thanks, and to offer to or receive a reward from a deity. The idea of fasting is to bring the body to an improved state deserving of a deity's reward.

Mysticism. Shamans and ancient priests fast to appease the anger of vengeful spirits or their deities. Primitive hunters fast to make themselves deserving of their quarry. And, the farmers fast for the earth and weather spirits to favor bountiful harvest.

Fasting for the Early Greeks

The early Greek people practiced fasting for health and therapeutic purposes. The Greek philosophers, such as Pythagoras, Hippocrates, Plato, Aristotle, Socrates, and Galen advocated fasting as a natural health remedy.

Paracelsus cited fasting as the 'physician within' referring to the internal mechanisms that protect the body system. Hippocrates, known as the father of medicine, prescribed the use of fasting and recommended taking apple cider vinegar. Plutarch supported fasting as a natural remedy instead of medicine. Pythagoras went on 40 days fast with water to sustain him, believing that abstaining from food results in enhanced creativity and mental perception.

The early Greeks believed in the natural healing capacity of man, much like nature, which is almost instinctual. For the early Greeks, fasting has a rejuvenating and revitalizing power.

Fasting in Religion

Fasting played a spiritual role in ancient religions; to this day, it remains a part of major religions worldwide. Jesus Christ, the prophet Muhammed, and Buddha shared the belief in fasting for health purposes and for the benefits it gives to the body. Fasting was also practiced spiritually for purification.

Traces of primitive rites of fasting can be seen in ancient and modern-day religious practices:

- The symbolic use of the unleavened bread by the Jews during the Passover traces back to the primitive rites
- Muslims' observance of fast by day and not after dark during Ramadan symbolizes penitence which is reminiscent of ancient practices
- Early Christians' fasting is symbolism for penitence and purification, which the primitive people did in preparation for offering their purified selves to a deity. The practice of fasting today is also done as preparation before receiving the sacraments of Holy Communion, baptism, and ordination of priests.

Modern-Day Fasting

Today, the original concept of fasting became modified and complicated. Fasting became complicated with the addition of other items, like juices instead of water, fruits, and other nutritious food. Technically, the modern concept of restrictions will fall under 'diets' which many refer to as 'cleansing' diets or 'detox diets.'

Regardless of the term used to mean fasting, there is hope for its health and therapeutic use.

Some healers and physicians with spiritual and holistic orientation recommend the use of fasting for health purposes. Conventional medicine does not fully recognize fasting as a natural health remedy. However, the idea of the body-mind connection is gradually taking hold in the field of modern-day medicine.

Physicians today are willing to accept fasting, not to interfere with the practice, but to build up the body's healing mechanisms. With this acceptance, fasting may recover its original concept as a self-healing mechanism of the body.

Currently, many researchers conduct studies on the unseen energy that naturally moves the body towards health and balance. Some physicians believe the field of medicine will encompass the study of the body's energy patterns. Knowledge obtained from these studies can enhance the energy patterns for a man's health and well-being.

The purpose of fasting varies, and the benefits you get when you fast are many. Physically, fasting is a natural resting period during which time the body eliminates the stored waste material so greater healing can happen. Spiritually, religious people believe that fasting provides the opportunity for clarity and insights that can lead to stronger faith and understanding.

Conclusion

We have gone through a comprehensive overview of what the intermittent fasting process is and how it is associated with autophagy. We've touched on the benefits of intermittent fasting in relation to autophagy, as well as some things to think about when considering this weight-loss method. Make sure you're aware of these things before beginning a fasting lifestyle that will secure the health benefits!

It's not every day that a diet becomes so popular that it even goes viral on social media. But that's exactly what happened recently when a Reddit user shared before-and-after photos of their transformation through intermittent fasting. This diet, which involves eating regularly for several days a week, and fasting the other days is touted as an effective way to lose weight and cut back on unhealthy cravings. While intermittent fasting may provide some benefits to overall health, it can also be dangerous if not done properly. Here, we explore why intermittent fasting is so popular and how the body's natural process of autophagy can support weight loss in a healthy manner.

Intermittent fasting is a concept that has been around since ancient times. When practiced correctly, it can be a helpful tool in managing weight and may even have some positive health benefits. However, as with any diet or lifestyle modification, it's important to discuss it with your doctor first to ensure that it is safe for you.

Intermittent fasting is an eating pattern which involves cycles of short periods of eating followed by longer periods where no food is consumed. There are various types of intermittent fasting regimens, including alternate day fasting and the 5:2 diet (which involves cutting calories on 2 days of the week and eating normally on the other days). Some people may even choose to eat all their food in a short window during the day. Regardless of which option you choose, the one common goal of intermittent fasting is to increase caloric restriction and encourage the body to burn fat.

Intermittent fasting has become increasingly popular over the last few years thanks to a growing number of research supporting its effectiveness in weight loss. It also has no adverse side effects on the body, unlike some traditional methods of calorie restriction, such as the Atkins diet.

The most well-known form of intermittent fasting is the 5:2 diet, which involves eating normally five days a week and consuming just 500 calories on two non-consecutive days each week. Another popular method is alternate day fasting, which involves eating normally one day and then consuming just 25% of the normal caloric intake on the following day.

Intermittent fasting is not the same as calorie restriction, which is a practice that involves decreasing the total number of calories you consume over a given period of time. Whereas intermittent fasting requires that you consume fewer calories on a given day (or several days); with calorie restriction, you are trying to cut back your overall caloric intake and eat less each day.

Despite conflicting research on the effectiveness of different methods of intermittent fasting, they all seem to have one characteristic in common: they seem to help promote weight loss in obese people. Studies suggest that eating cycles may affect our metabolism and increase fat burning by increasing energy expenditure.

When making dietary changes, it is always best to consult with a trained healthcare professional, even if you just change the timing when you eat food. An intermittent diet is one such diet. It claims to increase appetite and help with the treatment of cases of anorexia, bulimia, heart disease, and high blood pressure. The diet does not forbid the consumption of some foods but suggests that certain times of eating can be better for the body, for example:

- Eat breakfast within 60 minutes after waking up.
- Do not eat lunch in the 3–4 hours before going to bed.
- Eat a large dinner early in the evening, about 2–3 hours before bedtime.

It is possible to skip the dinner meal and sleep a little longer and still maintain a healthy weight and heart rate. An intermittent diet does not forbid the consumption of any food. However, it encourages changing the times of consumption for better health.

Use it as an effective tool for rising weight, lowering blood pressure, and enjoying a healthier heart. Intermittent fasting has many potential health benefits, and it is particularly promising in diabetes treatment and management. It is a good option for older adults to develop a healthier diet and lifestyle.

Remember: consult your doctor about your diet, especially if you have a history of certain medical conditions. They know your medical history and condition and are aware of your risks related to dietary changes. Work with them on achieving a healthy regimen that works best for you. An intermittent diet may be the way to go for you. It is essential to understand how incredibly smart our bodies are when it comes to fasting and dieting. When we look at the diets of many of the most successful people in history, this has been their way and it works! Try it!

A healthy eating plan for weight loss is to eat regularly but with small meals. Eating fewer meals a day may help you burn excess fat and maintain good health. Health experts recommend eating your last meal at least four hours before you sleep. This allows your body to store only the calories you need and release the rest as energy instead of storing all of it as fat.

It is common to see weight loss after 6 months of a diet, so stick with the plan. However, it is important to make changes slowly so that you don't feel hungry or suffer from malnutrition. The ideal diet for older adults is more flexible in order to take into account their lifestyle and eating habits. Instead of strict caloric consumption, an intermittent diet proposes more nutritious food at regular intervals throughout the day. By eating smaller, more frequent meals, a person can help their metabolism and nutrient absorption. This will help you reach your goal faster with less effort.

I hope you enjoyed reading Intermittent fasting and autophagy: The new method for weight loss and purification. It is the best cure to regenerate, stimulate self-healing, strengthen defenses, rejuvenate and improve memory and learn something from it.

Thank you for reading This book.
If you enjoyed it, please visit the site where you
Purchased it and write a brief review. Your Feedback is
important to me and will help other readers decide
whether to read the book too.

Thank You
Keli Bay

Printed in Great Britain
by Amazon

75680792R00102